MW01118481

John L. Crompton is Distinguished Professor of Recreation, Park and Tourism Sciences at Texas A&M University. His primary interests are in the areas of marketing and financing public leisure and tourism services. He is author or coauthor of seven books and a substantial number of articles and monographs about recreation, tourism, and marketing.

Crompton has conducted many workshops on Marketing and/or Financing Leisure Services. He has lectured or conducted workshops in a number of foreign countries and has delivered keynote addresses at the Annual National Park and Recreation Conferences in Great Britain, Canada, Australia, South Africa, New Zealand, and Japan.

He is a past recipient of the National Park Foundation's Cornelius Amory Pugsley award for outstanding national contributions to parks and conservation; the National Recreation and Park Association's (NRPA) National Literary Award; the NRPA's Roosevelt Award for outstanding research; the Distinguished Colleague Award and the Distinguished Teaching Award of the Society of Park and Recreation Educators; and the Travel and Tourism Research Association's Travel Research Award. He has received the Vice-Chancellor's Award for Excellence in Graduate Teaching at Texas A&M, and the Texas Agricultural Experiment Station's Faculty Fellow Award for exceptional research contributions. He is a past-president of four professional bodies: the Texas Recreation and Parks Society; the American Academy of Park and Recreation Administration; the Society of Park and Recreation Educators; and the Academy of Leisure Sciences. He is currently a member of the NRPA's Board of Trustees, and chair of the NRPA Southwest Regional Council.

This report is sponsored by the Wallace-Reader's Digest Funds, the Doris Duke Charitable Foundation, and the American Planning Association's City Parks Forum and the Planning Advisory Service. The opinions expressed in this report are solely those of the author and do not necessarily reflect the views of the sponsors.

Cover design by Toni Thanasouras Ellis.

This report is printed on recycled paper.

The Planning Advisory Service is a subscription service offered by the Research Department of the American Planning Association. Eight reports are produced each year. Subscribers also receive the PAS Memo each month and have use of the Inquiry Answering Service. Frank S. So, Executive Director; Sylvia Lewis, Publications Director; William Klein, Director of Research.

Planning Advisory Service Reports are produced in the Research Department of APA. James Hecimovich, Editor; Marya Morris, Assistant Editor; Lisa Barton, Design Associate.

© November 2001 by the American Planning Association. APA's publications office is at 122 S. Michigan Ave., Suite 1600, Chicago, IL 60603. E-mail: pasreports@planning.org. APA headquarters office is at 1776 Massachusetts Ave., N.W., Washington, DC 20036.

TABLE OF CONTENTS

Parks and Economic Development

John L. Crompton

Foreword

This Planning Advisory Service Report is the second of three reports sponsored, in part, by the City Parks Forum. The first report, *Parks, Recreation, and Open Space: A Twenty-First Century Agenda* by Alexander Garvin, PAS Report No. 497/498, was published in December 2000.

CPF is a fellowship of mayors, their park advisors, and community leaders that encourages collaboration, the sharing of information, and an exchange of ideas about the role of parks in communities. The American Planning Association administers the CPF program, which is made possible by support from the Wallace-Reader's Digest Funds and the Doris Duke Charitable Foundation. For more information about CPF, the forums already held, the mayors who have attended, and the parks programs that have benefited from CPF grants, go to APA's web site (www.planning.org/cpf), e-mail CPF's director, Mary Eysenbach, at cpf@planning.org, or call 312-431-9100.

APA developed CPF to reach out to mayors to persuade and encourage them to elevate the status of parks on their agendas and in their city's budget. CPF staff consulted with a number of parks advocates from around the country about the structure and content of the program. One of the issues that these advocates prominently mentioned was the need for a better explanation for mayors of what parks have been, what parks are, and what parks will need to be to be successful in the "new" economics and society of twenty-first century America.

Alex Garvin's report provided that historical analysis, documenting the on-again, off-again commitment of the American public and governments to public space and outlining a set of strategies for spotlighting the importance and value of public open space and ways to create more of it and maintain better what we have.

This report, *Parks and Economic Development* by John Crompton, will add another highly important building block to the argument for the value of public open space. And it will be another report that parks advocates should carry with them to help ensure that they receive a more open and enthusiastic reception when they present their program agendas to political and business leaders.

I remember very well John's opening presentation at the first City Parks Forum in New Orleans in November 1999. He asked the mayors attending that event and the rest of the audience, Who is the tourism industry? He noted that the term is bandied about constantly, but if you try to answer that question, you fumble for your answers. In fact, it's never quite clear who belongs to that industry. What is clear is that many have claimed to be part of it and have positioned themselves as economic development leaders and advocates.

What John suggests in this report is that, in fact, park advocates, including planners, need to understand how the work they do every day is part of that "tourism industry" and goes well beyond that to be a strong element in a community's economic development efforts. These advocates need to "reposition" their programs and their agencies to take advantage of the positive "buzz" that accompanies the association with economic development leaders.

John clearly makes the point that, beyond the aesthetic, social, and health benefits that we normally associate with parks, the creation and enhancement of places that improve the quality of life of citizens, business owners and their employees, and the senior citizens of a community have a measurable positive effect on the bottom line of government coffers and businesses. These programs and activities provide benefits not only for new people coming to a community through job relocation, visits, or retirement, but for the long-term residents of the community.

Although some of John's discussion is aimed at parks and recreation staffs, much of what he says is applicable to the programs and responsibilities of the local planning department. Clearly, he suggests that if it isn't currently applicable, the planning department should reposition itself to make it applicable. He is primarily discussing fiscal impact analysis for parks and open space and other aspects of urban design (e.g., tree planting, streetscapes, and undergrounding infrastructure)—all factors that are currently usually ignored in impact calculations. He makes the point in several places that investment in these community improvements is far less risky and has far more long-term communitywide value than tax incentives to attract new businesses. In the last part of Chapter 2, he extends that discussion to specifically take into account different methods that planners can employ to fund parks and open space acquisitions and development. These techniques are part of the development process and are familiar to planners. They include excess purchase and condemnation, special assessment districts, business improvement districts, tax increment financing, and exactions.

John knows the economic development benefits of parks and open space, and has developed and enhanced techniques to measure them. He is the author or coauthor of seven books and a number of articles and monographs on tourism, recreation, and marketing. His awards for his contributions to the fields of parks and conservation research are numerous (see the inside cover the report for his bio). Much of the research for this report is an extension of work that he has conducted during the past 10 years for the National Parks and Recreation Association.

I find one of the most fascinating studies in the book the Colorado study that John and a coauthor conducted to respond to criticisms of previous research about the decision-making process in job relocation (see pages 54 and 55 in Chapter 4). He designed a study to make certain that surveys and interviews about job relocation went to the person who, in fact, was responsible for decisions regarding relocation and, furthermore, that the relocation had indeed taken place.

The research findings that John offers throughout the report are not hypothetical arguments; rather, they are "hard," economic development data grounded in empirical research. We hope you find them enlightening and useful. More importantly, we hope that the agencies and individuals who are responsible for budgeting for your parks and open space agendas find them persuasive.

Jim Hecimovich
Chief Editor, PAS Reports

Preface

The rationale for this PAS Report is summarized in the following observation:

> Too many community leaders feel they must choose between economic growth and open space protection. But no such choice is necessary. Open space protection is good for a community's health, stability, beauty, and quality of life. It is also good for the bottom line (Rogers 1999, 3).

As contributors to the local economy, parks and open spaces are equal to roads, utilities, and other infrastructure elements. The cost of investing in these elements is justified by the economic value that derives from their availability. Unfortunately, many growing communities lack the foresight to set aside land for inclusion in a parks system in the same way as they do for other infrastructure elements. They frequently claim that resources are not available for what they regard as a discretionary investment. And in many built-out communities, vacant land is seen as a precious resource that needs to be developed to grow the tax base rather than as an opportunity to provide open space and park resources.

Public parks traditionally have not been evaluated in economic terms because there are many other appealing and rational justifications for acquiring and providing them. These may include:

(1) enhancement of a community's quality of life, which embraces its livability, "feel," and aesthetic integrity, and the role of parks and open spaces in creating a sense of place or community;

(2) ecological and environmental issues, including biological diversity, improving water quality, air cleansing, aquifer recharge, and flood control; and

(3) scenic vistas and places for engaging in active or passive recreation activities.

Although the primary purpose of park and recreation facilities may not be financial, financial justification for providing them is nearly always required. The difficult fiscal environment that prevails in many cities and the escalation of urban land values have made the economic justification of park land increasingly necessary in order to rebut the persuasive rhetoric of those who say "I am in favor of parks and open space, but we cannot afford either the capital acquisition and development costs because of more pressing priorities, or the loss of operational revenue if the land is removed from the tax rolls." If the flaws in this economic shibboleth are exposed and nullified, the likelihood of investments in parks using the traditional justifications noted in the numbered list above is enhanced.

The challenge is to achieve widespread recognition of the economic contribution of parks and to measure it, so that it is adequately represented in the planning, social, and political calculus of community infrastructure decisions. If park advocates are limited when making their case to general statements (e.g., "We know the presence of parks has a beautiful and beneficial effect on our community even though we cannot place a specific value on it."), they are likely to lose contests with developers for land. In contrast to such subjective generalities from conservationists, developers are likely to cite the specific increase in dollar value of the tax base that will accrue if a site is developed.

The first chapter in this report recognizes that the economic contributions of parks and open space currently are not widely recognized or understood by taxpayers or elected officials. To rectify this situation, a strategy based on the concept of repositioning is suggested.

The other chapters are concerned with two ways to measure the economic value of parks and recreation. The first way, described in Chapter 2, captures the capitalization worth of parks by measuring their impact on the value of land and property in their immediate catchment zone. The second type of measure is the economic value derived from visitors (Chapter 3), businesses (Chapter 4), and retirees (Chapter 5) whose decisions to come to the area are at least in part predicated on the availability of parks and recreation opportunities.

The use of these measures, however, will provide only a *minimum* estimate of the economic value of recreation and parks because these measures are not able to capture all dimensions of the benefits these amenities provide to a community. Benefits that are omitted from the calculus include such factors as air cleansing, groundwater storage, flood control, elimination of waste, alleviation of environmental stress, pleasing vistas, and the social capital stemming from rejuvenated and rehabilitated people.

CHAPTER 1

Repositioning Park and Recreation Services

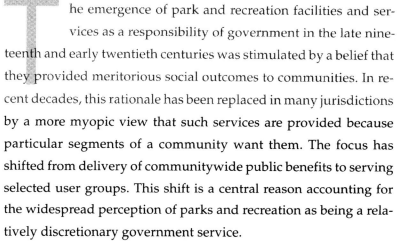

The emergence of park and recreation facilities and services as a responsibility of government in the late nineteenth and early twentieth centuries was stimulated by a belief that they provided meritorious social outcomes to communities. In recent decades, this rationale has been replaced in many jurisdictions by a more myopic view that such services are provided because particular segments of a community want them. The focus has shifted from delivery of communitywide public benefits to serving selected user groups. This shift is a central reason accounting for the widespread perception of parks and recreation as being a relatively discretionary government service.

Servicing user groups will always be a central element of the parks and recreation mission, but in many jurisdictions user groups are too narrow a constituency to justify sustaining or investing additional tax revenues in these services. User satisfaction, while necessary, is an inadequate indicator of the success of a park and recreation department when used alone, because it does not incorporate non-users' evaluations of the agency. Most taxpayers are not frequent users of these services. Thus, many of them have difficulty understanding why they should support them. This prevailing sentiment is often heard: If only some segments of our community use park and recreation services, why should the rest of us have to pay for them? To elicit the support of non-users, an agency has to provide a convincing answer to the fundamental marketing question, What is in it for them? Broader community support is likely to be dependent on building awareness not only of the on-site benefits that accrue to users, but also of the off-site communitywide benefits that accrue to non-users.

To elicit the support of non-users, an agency has to provide a convincing answer to the fundamental marketing question, What is in it for them?

TEN COLLECTIVE "PUBLIC" BENEFITS THAT MAY ACCRUE FROM PARK AND RECREATION SERVICES

Economic Development:

1) *Attracting Tourists:* The major factor considered by tourists when they make a decision about which communities to visit on a pleasure trip is the attractions that are available. In most cities, those attractions are dominated by facilities and services operated by park and recreation agencies and their non-profit partners (parks, beaches, events, festivals, athletic tournaments, museums, historical sites, cultural performances, etc.). Without such attractions, there is no tourism.

2) *Enhancing Real Estate Values:* People are prepared to pay more to live close to natural park areas. The enhanced value of these properties results in their owners paying higher property taxes to governments. If the incremental amount of taxes paid by each property that is attributable to the park is aggregated, it is often sufficient to pay the annual debt charges required to retire the bonds used to acquire and develop the park.

3) *Attracting Businesses:* In many cases, the viability of businesses in the highly recruited high-technology, research and development, company headquarters, and services sectors is dependent on their ability to attract and retain highly educated professional employees. The deciding factor of where these individuals choose to live is often the quality of life in the geographic vicinity of the business. No matter how quality of life is defined, park and recreation opportunities are likely to be a major component of it.

4) *Attracting Retirees:* A new clean growth industry in America today is the increasing number of relatively affluent, active retirees. Their decision as to where to locate with their substantial retirement incomes is primarily governed by two factors: climate and recreational opportunities.

Alleviating Social Problems:

5) *Preventing Youth Crime:* The use of park and recreation programs to alleviate youth crime was a primary political stimulant for much of the early recreation provision in major cities at the beginning of the twentieth century. There is strong evidence demonstrating the success of these programs when they are structured to provide social support from adult leaders; leadership opportunities for youth; intensive and individualized attention to participants; a sense of group belonging; youth input into program decisions; and opportunities for community service. The return on investment of such programs is substantial when compared with the costs of incarceration.

There is increased recognition that the "private" benefits that accrue to users are likely to have relatively little impact on resource allocation decisions made by elected officials. These benefits are described as "private" because they are enjoyed only by program participants and do not extend to the majority of the population who are only occasional users or non-users. Providing resources to a parks and recreation department so a minority of residents can have enjoyable experiences is likely to be a low priority when measured against the critical economic, health, safety and welfare issues with which most legislative bodies are confronted.

"PUBLIC" BENEFITS *(cont'd)*

6) *Healthy Lifestyles:* There is growing recognition that the key to curtailing health care costs lies in prevention of illness so it does not have to be treated by the expensive medical system. Park and recreation services contribute to this end not only by facilitating improvements in physical fitness through exercise, but also by facilitating positive emotional, intellectual, and social experiences. People with high levels of wellness have a proclivity to act during their free time, rather than merely be acted on.

7) *Environmental Stress:* Environmental stress may involve both psychological emotions (e.g., frustrations, anger, fear and coping responses) and associated physiological responses that use energy and contribute to fatigue. It is experienced daily by many who live or commute in urban or blighted areas. Parks in urban settings have a restorative effect that releases the tensions of modern life. Evidence demonstrating the therapeutic value of natural settings has emerged in both physiological and psychological studies. The cost of environmental stress in terms of work days lost and medical care is likely to be substantially greater than the cost of providing and maintaining parks, urban forestry programs, and oases of flowers and shrubs.

8) *Unemployment and Underemployment:* Basic psychological needs that many people derive from their work are difficult to acquire when they are working in low-level service jobs such as cashiers, janitors, and cleaners, which are the major growth positions in the economy. And, of course, if they are unemployed, such needs may be totally unmet. These include self-esteem, prestige accruing from peer group recognition, ego satisfaction of achievement, a desire to be successful, excitement and self-worth. For the growing number of people in low-level jobs, these needs will be fulfilled in their familial or leisure milieus, or they will not be fulfilled at all.

Environmental Stewardship:

9) *Historical Preservation:* Without a cultural history, people are rootless. Preserving historical remnants offers lingering evidence to remind people of what they once were, who they are, what they are, and where they are. It feeds their sense of history.

10) *The Natural Environment:* People turn to the natural environment, preserved by humans as a park, wilderness, or wildlife refuge, for something they cannot get in a built environment. The quality of human life depends on an ecologically sustainable and aesthetically pleasing physical environment. The surge of interest in conserving open spaces by people motivated by ecological and aesthetic concerns is matched by a similar surge from those concerned that the inexorable rise in demands for outdoor recreation is not being matched by a commensurate expansion of the supply base. ■

To justify the investment of additional resources, elected officials have to be convinced—as they were in an earlier era—that park and recreation agencies deliver collective or "public" benefits. Public benefits are defined as those that accrue to most people in a community, even if some people in a community do not participate in an agency's programs or use its facilities.

The sidebar above suggests 10 public benefits that may accrue from park and recreation services. They are classified into three broad categories: economic development, alleviating social problems, and environmental stewardship. The task of those responsible for parks, open space, and recreation is to identify which of these public benefits are most prominent on a jurisdiction's political agenda and to demonstrate their agency's or organization's potential contribution to fulfilling that agenda. This publication focuses on four potential contributions that the various park and recreation resources (and the agencies that help make them possible) may make to economic development. That is not to say that the other items in the list are not as important; it is simply that the author's expertise is in the area of the relationship between parks and economic development—an area with less "quantifiable" research than some of the others in the list. The afterword to this report, written by the director of APA's City Parks Forum, comments on the difficulties of doing research that quantifies the value of all the many benefits of parks.

The contributions that can be made to economic development by parks, open space, and recreation resources and that are the focus of this report are:

When you think in terms of aligning parks issues with a politically important issue, such as economic development, you are embracing a concept termed positioning.

- enhancing real estate values;

- attracting tourists;

- attracting businesses;

- attracting retirees.

Economic development is a political priority in most communities because it is viewed as a means of enlarging the tax base. The enlargement provides more tax revenues that governments can use either to improve the community's infrastructure, facilities, and services, or to reduce the level of taxes paid by existing residents. It is seen also as a source of jobs and income that enables residents to improve their quality of life.

THE CONCEPT OF POSITIONING

When you think in terms of aligning parks issues with a politically important issue, such as economic development, you are embracing a concept termed positioning. Positioning refers to the place that parks and their related activities occupy in the minds of elected officials and the general public relative to their perception of other services that are "competitors" for public tax dollars.

Without competition, positioning would be unnecessary and a good image would probably suffice to attract support and resources. Most park and recreation agencies have a positive image in their communities. Surveys invariably report an overwhelming percentage of residents as being "satisfied" or "very satisfied" with an agency's performance. Often, however, this does not translate into increased resources because the agency's performance and importance are evaluated in isolation and are not related to the performance and importance of other agencies with which it is competing for funds. Thinking in terms of position rather than image is more useful because it embraces comparison with competitors. It compares elected officials' and taxpayers' perceptions of the park and recreation agency with those they hold of other public services in which they may invest.

Identifying and establishing a strong, preferred position is the most important strategic decision that park advocates make. This identification is likely to determine an agency's or organization's future. Once the decision has been made, all subsequent actions should be geared to implementing it. An established position that reflects responsiveness to a community's central concerns is the key for an agency to:

- develop and nurture a broader constituency;

- secure additional resources;

- guide programmatic and facility priorities made by staff and stakeholders; and

- improve the morale of staff by raising their perceived status in the community.

The goal should be to reinforce the desired position by integrating as many of the agency's actions as possible, so each component action fulfills a role in helping to establish the position in the minds of stakeholders.

The position of park and recreation services that has existed in the minds of most stakeholders for several decades is that they are relatively discretionary, nonessential services. They are nice to have if they can be afforded after the important, essential services have been funded. Driver and Bruns (1999, 351) observed that:

> Elected officials in the United States and Canada tend to hold the erroneous belief that most to all of the benefits of leisure accrue to the individuals who use leisure services and that there are few to any spin-off benefits from this use to society in general. This contrasts with their views about the social merits of other social services (e.g., education, health services, police and fire protection, transportation) for which these elected officials acknowledge large benefits to society beyond those that accrue to the direct users of those services. Therefore, these officials have improperly adopted for leisure services the principle of public finance, which dictates that only limited public funds should be allocated to a social service that does not promote the general welfare.

Thus, the key to securing additional resources for park and recreation services is to reposition them so they are perceived as helping to alleviate the problems that are the prevailing political concerns of policy makers responsible for allocating tax funds. Only when they are so repositioned will park and recreation services be perceived positively as part of the solution to a jurisdiction's problems, rather than as having no impact or even as a drain on tax resources.

Problem issues will differ across communities, but the following list suggests some of the most common that are likely to emerge:

- Economic development

- Alleviation of youth crime

- Reduction of health care costs

- Improved standards of education

- Watershed protection

- Flooding protection

- Unemployment

- Quality of life

- Air/Water pollution

- Downtown redevelopment

These are the issues likely to surface in election campaigns, indicating that they are of primary concern to residents. Hence, officials who are elected on a platform promising to address one or more of these priority issues are

The key to securing additional resources for park and recreation services is to reposition them so they are perceived as helping to alleviate the problems that are the prevailing political concerns of policy makers responsible for allocating tax funds.

Mary Eysenbach

mandated to direct resources towards them. If park and recreation services are to receive a share of these resources, they must address these key problems and demonstrate that they can contribute to alleviating them.

Which issue(s) an agency or organization elects to focus on depends on the community's priorities and the personnel and facility resources available to that agency or organization. The preferred position should be the optimum "selling idea" in order to motivate taxpayers and elected officials to allocate additional resources for parks and recreation. *A cardinal rule, however, is that an agency or organization should position itself by aligning with only one or at the very most two community issues because establishing a position in residents' minds requires prolonged focus.*

To residents, perceptions are truth. Their perceptions may not be correct, especially those of nonusers who have little contact with parks and their programs, but it is what they know, and they have no reason to make an effort to know more. Most taxpayers, therefore, are unlikely to pay much attention to the details, subtleties, and complexities of the roles that the principal agencies and organizations for parks acquisition, development, and programming may make.

In the age of the "sound bite," focus is everything. The message offered by park advocates has to be focused, consistent, and pervasive.

In the age of the "sound bite," focus is everything. The message offered by park advocates has to be focused, consistent, and pervasive. The best they can hope for is that an occasional piece of information is widely dispersed and reinforces residents' positive image of parks or changes the perception of those who consider them unimportant.

The value of consistency over time in program emphasis and in communications cannot be overemphasized. If you do not concentrate your resources to support a focused repositioning strategy, it will not succeed. The probable outcome of diffusing resources and the message by aligning with multiple issues is that no clear identity will be established. Consequently, the message will only confuse the public, perhaps making a bad situation worse.

Repositioning is a difficult task because it involves changing a widely held, long-established public attitude (and maybe even the attitude of the staff of the organization that is being repositioned). Furthermore, there are pragmatic difficulties in shifting to align with a selected key issue. An agency or organization cannot immediately abandon many of its current tasks and switch resources to strengthen its repositioning efforts. If this were done, there would probably be a loud outcry from existing clientele. Such shifts can only be implemented over time.

Agencies, therefore, should think in terms of a 10-year, rather than a 1-year, time horizon to accomplish repositioning. For planners, the repositioning strategy timetable might coincide with the term of the comprehensive plan or a redefined open space element. After all, it probably took at least 10 years for some of the public to come to the conclusion that parks are nonessential and that discretionary spending on them should be minimized; it may take at least that long to change that position in those minds.

THE SET OF REPOSITIONING STRATEGIES

Parks advocates and their agencies and organizations can pursue three strategies to achieve repositioning. The strategies are not mutually exclusive; rather, all three should be embraced simultaneously.

Real Repositioning

The first strategy is real repositioning, which means that an agency or organization changes what it does so that its work meets a community's priorities. For example, adopting a more aggressive entrepreneurial approach to soliciting tourism business for the community (see sidebar on facing page).

Real repositioning may involve not only changing program offerings, but also changing the types of alliances and partnerships that an agency or organization forms. It may mean changing the community forums in which it becomes involved. Allying with other agencies or organizations that already have a well-crystallized image and position may provide a "reference point" for a new position in the mind of the public and elected officials. For instance, strengthening links with a jurisdiction's tourism agency may be an effective repositioning strategy. If the tourism agency holds a positive position in stakeholders' minds, closer links with it are likely to lead to some of its positive position being conveyed by association.

Real repositioning could involve actively partnering with the community tourism agency to create new events designed to attract outside visitors to stay in the jurisdiction for multiple days. Such linkages make pragmatic sense because two organizations often have complementary assets. Tourism agencies typically have funds available for promotion, whereas such funds may be scarce at most planning and park and recreation agencies. In contrast, tourism agencies rarely become involved in directly producing programs and services. Some departments, for example, cooperate with tourism agencies to fund coordinators who are responsible for organizing and soliciting sponsorship for special events in the community. The tourism agencies recognize that planning departments and park and recreation departments have the expertise and a mandate to organize special events, but frequently lack the funds to launch and promote them effectively. Hence, tourism agencies help fund such positions, provide initial seed funds for some events, and promote all events.

Real repositioning is the foundation upon which all action rests. An agency must not try to be something it is not. It is important that it is able to deliver the outcomes it promises. If an agency or organization aligns with economic development, it must structure its services and engage in cooperative partnerships that are compatible with that new alignment.

Competitive Repositioning

The second strategy is competitive repositioning. This means altering stakeholders' beliefs about what an agency's competitors do. For example, consider the local convention and visitors bureau. Its principal job is to attract visitors. The bureau will frequently imply that the economic impact from all visitors is attributable to its efforts. In this way, it has positioned itself in the minds of stakeholders as an important contributor to economic development, and it receives resources commensurate with that favorable position. As will become clear in chapter 2, this substantially overstates the contribution because many visitors would come even if there were no convention and visitors bureau, while others are there because of the efforts of park advocates and their agencies and organizations rather than those of the bureau. If the discrepancies in the relationship between the "value" of a bureau's claimed contributions and that value in reality are subtly pointed out, resources that would otherwise be appropriated to the bureau may instead be allocated to an agency or agencies that is or can become a principal actor in developing additional events or facilities to attract visitors.

Psychological Repositioning

Psychological repositioning is the third strategy. This type of repositioning means altering stakeholders' beliefs about what an agency currently does. The activities and facilities provided by planning and parks and recreation agencies and organizations already attract an extensive number of visitors to a community. In these cases, the primary strategy should be psychological repositioning, which involves documenting, demonstrating, and inform-

AN ENTREPRENEURIAL APPROACH TO ATTRACTING TOURISTS

An agency could develop packaged services for visitors. For example, in every area there are numerous organizations that have a program chair whose challenge is to develop a program of activities for the group. Park and recreation agencies have a smorgasbord of offerings available to meet those groups' programming needs. Managing facilities and services does not stop at the front gate! The challenge is not merely to provide services that people want; it is to package them so they can be accessed conveniently.

Packaging means that the agency links with a transportation source and necessary support services, such as a restaurant and hotel (if an overnight stay is involved), and offers a fixed price for the total experience to targeted groups. Thus, if an agency offers a fishing trip to senior citizen groups, the package may include a chartered bus, lunch, fishing poles, and a staff person who meets the chartered bus and provides interpretation and assistance with bait, fishing, cleaning fish, and so forth. Targeting groups from outside of the community with packages would help to reposition an agency as a central contributor to tourism and economic development.

AN ILLUSTRATION OF PSYCHOLOGICAL REPOSITIONING

The city council could not be persuaded to commit $1.5 million to purchase land for a 150-acre youth athletic field complex for which there was a clearly demonstrated need. The proposed site was adjacent to two major highways and would be well suited for tournaments in such sports as soccer, rugby, baseball, softball, tennis, and lacrosse. However, the city did have resources to invest in economic development projects. Hence, after an initial rejection by the council, the project's supporters regrouped and repositioned the project as an outdoor special-events center.

This terminology resonated with the council and taxpayers because the city had both an existing indoor special-events center and a conference center, and they were recognized widely to be good investments in economic development because of the nonresident visitors they attracted. Representatives of the hotel-motel association, restaurant association, convention and visitors bureau, and chamber of commerce came to a council meeting to lobby for the athletic complex because its supporters pointed out that the city could hold frequent tournaments bringing 300 to 500 people to the community each weekend from out of town.

Once it was repositioned into this economic development context and viewed as an outdoor special-events center, the council approved resources to acquire the site. They also recommended that some hotel-motel tax funds be used for this purpose, reducing the amount needed from taxpayers.

ing stakeholders of the economic benefits that accrue from those activities and facilities. The results of such studies may be viewed as interesting and newsworthy, which would facilitate communication of them by the media to stakeholders.

Godbey (1993) has suggested that park and recreation agencies, in particular, have a labeling problem. Agencies are labeled based on the means used (i.e., recreation), rather than the ends that they aspire to achieve (e.g., contributing to economic development). In the past two decades, emphasis was placed on providing the means, while the ends were forgotten.

Psychological repositioning involves bringing outcomes to the forefront so that when the words "parks and recreation" are mentioned, people immediately think of them as wanted outcomes or benefits. This is illustrated effectively in the area of tourism where public investments in promoting tourism or developing new tourism opportunities are associated in people's minds with economic development, which most people and politicians consider to be a highly desirable outcome.

Another strategy for psychological repositioning is to take advantage of the positive position that tourism organizations in many communities have established in stakeholders' minds by making extensive use of the vocabulary of "tourism." The extreme case would be a change in a department's name that better reflected that agency's central contribution to tourism in the community. If political considerations make such a change infeasible, consistent reference to an agency's active role in the "recreation and tourism industry" and to its "tourism" services may enable it to build a bridge to tourism's established position. Over time, this is likely to lead to some of the positive associations with tourism for that agency.

CHAPTER 2

The Impact of Parks and Open Space on Real Estate Values and the Property Tax Base

The real estate market consistently demonstrates that many people are willing to pay a higher price for a property located close to parks and open space areas than for a home that does not offer this amenity. The higher value of these residences means that their owners pay higher property taxes. In effect, this represents a "capitalization" of parkland into increased property values for proximate landowners.

This effect was widely acknowledged from the early days of urban park development in the latter half of the nineteenth century. Frederick Law Olmsted was able to articulate this effect and to persuade elected officials in New York City to invest the almost $14 million required to construct Central Park. After listening to Olmsted's argument, the New York City Comptroller, writing in 1856 shortly after the city acquired title to the land for Central Park, said "the increase in taxes by reason of the enhancement of values attributable to the park would afford more than sufficient means for the interest incurred for its purchase and improvement without any increase in the general rate of taxation" (Metropolitan Conference 1928, 12).

Olmsted verified the principle of capitalization in the case of Central Park by subsequently providing empirical evidence of it (Fox 1990). He was responsible for the earliest documentation of the relationship between public parks and real estate values. This documentation was widely disseminated and was a powerful weapon in the armory of early public and open space advocates seeking to persuade communities to commit new investments in these amenities.

Olmsted verified the principle of capitalization in the case of Central Park by subsequently providing empirical evidence of it. (Fox 1990)

THE BASIC PRINCIPLE—THE PROXIMATE PRINCIPLE

This process of capitalization is termed the "proximate principle." It means that, in some instances, the increase in property values in an area due to the presence of a park leads to higher property taxes. Those higher taxes have been shown in some cases to provide sufficient funds to pay the annual debt charges on the bonds used to acquire and develop the park. When this happens, the park is obtained at no long-term cost to the jurisdiction.

This principle is illustrated in the hypothetical 50-acre park shown in Figure 2-1. It is a natural, resource-oriented park with some appealing topography and vegetation. The cost of acquiring and developing it (fencing, trails, supplementary planting, some landscaping) is $20,000 an acre, so the total capital cost is $1 million. The annual debt charges for a 20-year general obligation bond on $1 million at 5 percent are approximately $90,000.

FIGURE 2-1. Layout of a 50-acre natural park and the proximate neighborhood Area

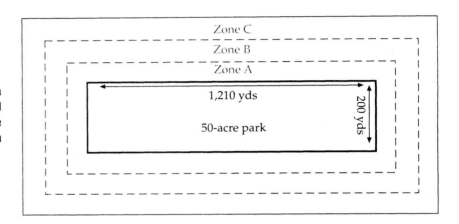

A projected annual income stream to service the bond debt was calculated as follows:

1) If properties around the park were 2,000-square-foot homes on half-acre lots (40 yards by 60 yards) with 40-yard frontages on the park, there would be 70 lots in Zone A (30 lots along each of the 1,210-yard perimeters, and 5 lots along each of the 200-yard perimeters).

2) Assume total property taxes payable to city, county, and school district are 2 percent of the market value of the property.

3) Assume the market value of similar properties elsewhere in the jurisdiction beyond the immediate influence of this park is $200,000.

4) Assume the desire to live close to a large natural park creates a willingness to pay a premium of 20 percent for properties in Zone A; 10 percent in Zone B; and 5 percent, in Zone C, and that there are also 70 lots in Zones B and C. A review of empirical studies that have investigated this issue suggests these values as a "point of departure" (Crompton 2001a, 3).

Table 2-1 shows that, given the above assumptions, the annual incremental property tax payments in the three zones from the premiums attributable to the presence of the park amount to $98,000. This is sufficient to pay the $90,000 annual bond debt charges.

Zone	Market value of each home	Incremental value attributed to the park	Total property taxes at 2%	Incremental property taxes attributed to the park	Aggregate amount of property tax increments given 70 home sites
Outside the park's influence	$200,000	$0	$4,000	$0	$0
A (20% premium)	$240,000	$40,000	$4,800	$800	$56,000
B (10% premium)	$220,000	$20,000	$4,400	$400	$28,000
C (5% premium)	$210,000	$10,000	$4,200	$200	<u>$14,000</u>
					$98,000

TABLE 2-1. How property taxes pay the annual debt for acquisitions and the development of the park.

The flows of this investment cycle are shown in Figure 2-2:

1) The council invests $90,000 a year for 20 years (annual debt charges on a $1 million bond) to construct or renovate a park,

2) causing the values of properties proximate to the park to increase,

3) leading to higher taxes paid by the proximate property owners to the council,

4) which are sufficient to fully reimburse the $90,000 annual financial investment made by the council.

Four additional points are worth noting that may further strengthen the economic case.

First, this illustration assumes no state or federal grants are available to aid in the park's acquisition and development. If they were available to reduce the community's capital outlay, the incremental property tax income stream would greatly exceed what was required to service the debt payments.

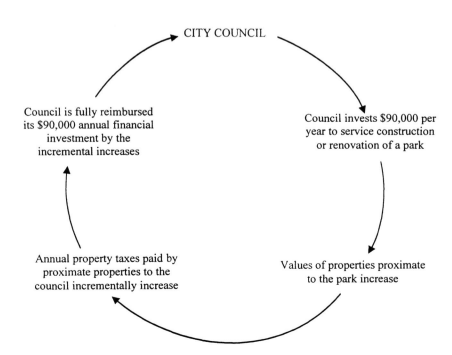

CITY COUNCIL

Council is fully reimbursed its $90,000 annual financial investment by the incremental increases

Council invests $90,000 per year to service construction or renovation of a park

Annual property taxes paid by proximate properties to the council incrementally increase

Values of properties proximate to the park increase

FIGURE 2-2. The investment cycle associated with a local government's investment in a park.

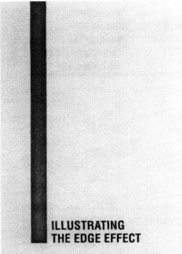

ILLUSTRATING THE EDGE EFFECT

A circular park that is 100 acres in area will have a radius of 1,177.8 feet. Given that the circumference of a circle is two times pi, times the radius, the amount of edge will be 7,396.7 feet.

Assume this park is unpeeled into a long strip of green that is one square acre wide (209 feet) — in effect, laying one acre next to another in a line. To find the length of the edge of 100 acres in this configuration, 209 feet is multiplied by 100 times 2, since there are 2 sides to this strip. The result is 41,800 linear feet, 5.65 times as much edge compared with a circular park of the same number of acres. That is the edge effect. ■

Source: Little (1990)

Second, the incremental property tax income will continue to accrue to the community after the 20-year period during which the debt charges will be repaid, at which time the net return to the community will be substantially enhanced.

Third, evidence suggests that investment in parks affects the comparative advantage of a community in attracting future businesses and desirable residential relocators, such as retirees. (This is discussed in Chapters 4 and 5.) The proximate capitalization approach, however, does not capture the secondary economic benefits attributable to park provision that accrue from such sources.

Finally, a park of the size shown in Figure 2-1 is likely to improve the quality of life and, thus, have some economic value to urban residents living beyond Zone C. The empirical data suggest that the capitalization of benefits ceases at a selected distance, usually somewhere between 500 feet and 3,000 feet away from the park perimeter in urban contexts (Crompton 2001a). It is unlikely, however, that park users and beneficiaries will be restricted to only those individuals located within such a narrowly defined service area.

The underestimation of economic benefit that occurs because some park users live outside a specified perimeter was demonstrated in a study of four parks containing a total of 219 acres in Worcester, Massachusetts (Allen, Stevens, and More 1985). The parks' zones of influence were terminated at 2,000 feet because the influence of the parks could not be clearly separated from numerous other elements influencing property values beyond that distance. When researchers conducted on-site interviews in the parks, however, between 51 percent and 75 percent of the parks' users lived outside the 2000-foot radius. Thus, the benefits accruing to these users were not represented in the economic benefit capitalization calculations.

A determining factor of the magnitude of a park's impact on the property tax base is the extent of the park's circumference or edge (Little 1990). If a 100-acre park is circular in shape, it has a relatively small circumference. If the 100 acres is distributed more linearly, the amount of edge increases substantially. The principle is illustrated by the calculations in the sidebar. The increased amount of edge means that more property can be sited adjacent to the park and the aggregate enhancement value of the property tax base is likely to be larger. This edge principle has been widely embraced in the design of golf courses incorporated into residential real estate developments. These are illustrated in Figure 2-3.

The almost rectangular shape of the core golf course is similar to the shape of traditional parks and has relatively little edge. The single fairway configurations have most edge and can accommodate the most real estate frontage (Muirhead and Rando 1994).

The preferred golf course option in most real estate developments is the single-fairway, "returning nines" configuration. This yields almost the maximum frontage for real estate and offers greater flexibility and efficiency in operation over the single-fairway continuous configuration by providing two starting holes. In other words, more players can begin a game, and the entire course can be brought into play in two hours, compared to four hours in a continuous layout with only one starting hole. Furthermore, this layout allows for the option of playing only nine holes (Muirhead and Rando 1994).

Approximately half of the golf courses constructed in the 1990s were associated with real estate developments (Dugas 1997). The appeal of golf course communities is not confined to golfers. Indeed, only approximately one-third of those who purchase houses in these developments play golf regularly (McElyea, Anderson, and Krekorian 1991). For the majority of

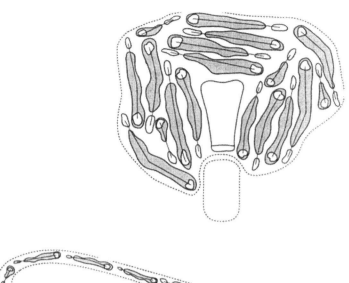

FIGURE 2-3. The Five Basic Golf Course Configurations

The Core Golf Course. Holes are clustered together, either in a continuous sequence, leaving the clubhouse at hole number 1 and returning to it a hole number 18, or in two returning nine-hole sequences, with each nine-hole sequence beginning and ending near the clubhouse. Because it consumes the least amount of land, the core course is usually the least expensive to build. However, the only sites it provides for real estate development lie at its perimeter. Length of available lot frontage is ±10,000 feet.

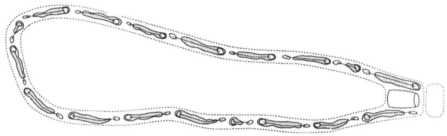

The Single Fairway, Continuous is a single, open loop starting from and returning to the clubhouse. Consumes the greatest amount of land and offers the greatest amount of fairway frontage for development sites, and can be designed to wind its way through fairly difficult terrain. Length of available lot frontage is ± 47,000 feet.

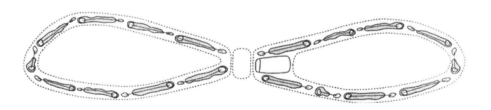

The Single Fairway, Returning Nines configuration consists of two loops of returning nines, with the clubhouse in the center. Most flexible for play, slightly less frontage due to the concentration of tees and greens for holes 1, 9, 10, and 18. Length of available lot frontage is ± 44,000 feet.

The Double Fairway, Continuous configuration consists of a continuous loop of adjacent, parallel fairways and offers about 40 percent less frontage for development sites than a single-fairway course, resulting in a boring course design. But the greater distance it provides from building sites on the opposite side of the fairway create a greater sense of spaciousness than does a single fairway lined by development. Length of available lot frontage is ± 25,000 feet.

Source: Muirhead and Rando (1994)

The Double Fairway, Returning Nines is characterized by two circuits of nine holes each, which both start and finish at the clubhouse, and both have adjacent parallel fairways. Length of available lot frontage is ± 24,000 feet.

homebuyers, the appeal is the open space and parklike ambiance that golf courses provide.

The developers' strategy mirrors the one advocated by Olmsted; namely, parks and selected recreation features are an investment, not a cost, because they generate more property taxes for a city (or added lot value for a developer) than they cost to service the annual debt charges incurred in creating the amenities. The high visibility, large number, and success of these golf course developments demonstrates by analogy to governmental stakeholders and decision makers that commercial developers implicitly recognize that recreation amenities and parklike open spaces enhance the surrounding land values sufficiently to offset their costs of acquisition and development. When using the golf course analogy, one must be prepared to make clear that it is the open space, views, and landscaping that add most value, not the fact that golf is played in the space.

POTENTIAL NEGATIVE INFLUENCES OF PARKS ON PROPERTY VALUES

Some types of parks are more desirable than others as places to live nearby. For example, there is convincing evidence that large flat open spaces used primarily for athletic activities and large social gatherings are much less preferred than natural areas containing woods, hills, ponds, or marsh (Kaplan and Kaplan 1990). Furthermore, it must be recognized that there are contexts in which parks exert a negative influence on property values. A useful analogy is with a well-groomed front lawn that is likely to increase the value of a home. If that lawn is overgrown with weeds, however, the property value is likely to be diminished (Fox 1990).

Adverse impacts may result from nuisances, such as:

- congestion;

- street parking;

- litter and vandalism that may occur due to the influx of people coming into a neighborhood to use a park;

- noise and ballfield lights may "intrude" on adjacent residences;

- poorly maintained or blighted, derelict facilities; and

- groups congregating in a park engaging in offensive activities.

There is convincing evidence that large flat open spaces used primarily for athletic activities and large social gatherings are much less preferred than natural areas containing woods, hills, ponds, or marsh.

Kaplan and Kaplan (1990)

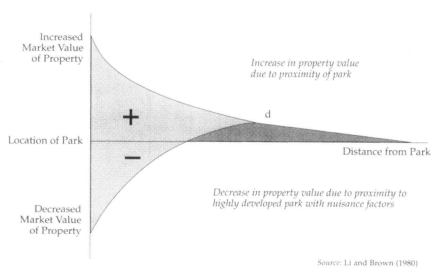

FIGURE 2–4. The positive and negative impacts of parks on residential property values.

Increased Market Value of Property

Increase in property value due to proximity of park

Location of Park

Distance from Park

Decrease in property value due to proximity to highly developed park with nuisance factors

Decreased Market Value of Property

Source: Li and Brown (1980)

Figure 2-4 recognizes that both positive and negative impacts on property values are possible. The top half of Figure 2-4 indicates that property value benefit increments associated with proximity and accessibility will decay as distance from the park increases. The lower half of Figure 2-4 suggests that any negative values are likely to be limited to properties in close proximity to the park, and these effects will decay more rapidly than positive impacts as distance from the park increases (Li and Brown 1980). Thus, in the negative scenario, property in the park's service area but beyond, for example, 500 feet is still likely to experience an increase in value because some benefits of access to the park's amenities accrue to these homeowners, but they avoid the nuisance costs inflicted on those who live close to it.

THE EMPIRICAL EVIDENCE ON THE PROXIMATE PRINCIPLE FOR PARKS AND OPEN SPACE

Olmsted's evidence from Central Park established the proximate principle as conventional wisdom among planners and park advocates, and resulted in it being used to justify major park investments in New York City and in many other communities in the early years of urban park development. For example, in a letter to the *New York Times* in 1882, a correspondent noted that Central Park "has not only paid, but it has been a most profitable investment, and regarded in the light of a real estate transaction alone, it has been a great success." He went on to observe that "those who want a reduction in the tax rate and those who favor the movement for its effect on real estate" were now "certain" to support development of future parks. As a result of the Central Park success, the letter writer advocated a proposal to acquire and develop two new 2,000-acre parks on the periphery of the city before its expanding population reached those areas. He argued:

> Four or five millions of dollars at the utmost will be sufficient and, as experience has proved, the City will not only be reimbursed for the outlay, but will receive in the increased tax income collected on the enhanced value of land contiguous to the proposed parks much more than will be required for maintenance and other accounts, leaving, as in the case of Central Park, a handsome profit on the investment.

Similar arguments were used in many other locales as local governments realized that large public parks encouraged new residential development on the periphery of a city. They believed this development expanded and strengthened the tax base (Fox 1990). Land on the fringes was inexpensive, and there was general acceptance of the principle that the increased tax revenue fully reimbursed the initial investment required to acquire and develop the land.

For approximately a century, from the earliest days of urban park development in the 1850s through the 1960s, there was an insistent, almost inviolate conviction among park advocates of the legitimacy of the proximate principle. It was conventional wisdom among them and was also widely espoused by elected officials.

During this time period, a number of other studies confirmed Olmsted's findings and reinforced the conventional wisdom. However, these early studies were fairly naive, reflecting the underdeveloped nature of the statistical tools and research designs available in the first half of the twentieth century. All property value increases were attributed to the proximity of a park and the potential influences of other factors were ignored, such as house age and size; lot size; distance to city center or major shopping center; and access to other amenities (e.g., schools and health care facilities). Although historical perspective suggests the findings reported by these studies may have been exaggerated because of their design failings, they illustrate the rich historical pedigree and tradition of the proximate principle and its effectiveness in persuading decision makers to invest in parks.

The limitations of the early studies were much better controlled in empirical studies undertaken after 1960. In these studies, property prices or assessed valuations were usually regressed against a measure of distance and a set of "control variables" that measured the contributions of other potential influences on property value as well as the influence of parks and open space. The increased sophistication of computing made feasible more complex analyses containing a greater number of control variables. The key questions these analyses addressed were:

A review of the results of 25 studies . . . indicated that, in 20 of them, parks and open space did contribute to increasing property values.

- Did parks and open space contribute to increasing property values when other potential influences on those values were also taken into account?

- How large was the proximate effect?

- Over what distance does the effect extend?

A review of the results of 25 studies that investigated the first issue indicated that, in 20 of them, parks and open space did contribute to increasing property values (Crompton 2001a). The support extended beyond urban areas to include properties that were proximate to large state parks, forests, and open space in rural areas. The rural studies offered empirical evidence to support not only the proximate principle, but also to refute the conventional wisdom that creating large state or federal park or forest areas results in a net reduction in the value of an area's tax base.

Six of the supportive studies further investigated whether there were differences in the magnitude of impact among parks with different design features and different types of uses. The findings demonstrated that parks serving primarily active recreation areas were likely to show much smaller proximate value increases than those accommodating only passive use. However, even with the noise, nuisance, and congestion emanating from active users, in most cases proximate properties tended to show increases in value when compared to properties outside a park's service zone. Impacts on proximate values were not likely to be positive in those cases where:

1) a park was not well maintained;

2) a park was not easily visible from nearby streets and, thus, provided opportunities for anti-social behavior; and

3) the privacy of properties backing on to a linear park was compromised by park users.

Examination of the five studies that did not support the proximate principle suggested that, in four of those cases, the ambivalent findings might have been attributable to methodological limitations.

The second question is related to the magnitude of the proximate effect. A definitive, general answer was not feasible given the substantial variation in the size, use, and design of parklands in the studies and the disparity in the residential areas around them. Since some point of departure based on the findings is needed for decision makers, however, Crompton (2001a, 62) suggests that:

> A positive impact of 20 percent on property values abutting or fronting a passive park area is a reasonable starting point guideline. If the park is large (say over 25 acres), well maintained, attractive, and its use is mainly passive, then this figure is likely to be low. If it is small and embraces some active use, then this guideline is likely to be high. If it is a heavily used

park incorporating such recreation facilities as athletic fields or a swimming pool, then the proximate value increment may be minimal on abutting properties but may reach 10 percent on properties two or three blocks away.

Likewise, it is not possible to offer a general, definitive answer to the question about the distance over which the proximate impact of parkland and open space extends. There appeared, however, to be wide agreement that it had substantial impact up to 500 feet and that, in the case of community-size parks (i.e., parks of approximately 40 acres or more), the proximate impact of a park was extended out to 2,000 feet. Few studies try to measure impacts beyond that distance because they become only one impact in a larger group of variables that come into play, and each of those variables compounds the complexity of the analysis. Nevertheless, in the case of these large parks, there was evidence to suggest impact beyond this artificial peripheral boundary because users of the park clearly came from beyond that boundary.

It is not possible to offer a general, definitive answer to the question about the distance over which the proximate impact of parkland and open space extends.

THE EMPIRICAL EVIDENCE ON THE PROXIMATE PRINCIPLE FOR GREENWAYS

In the 1990s, there was an explosion of interest in developing greenways. Greenways are corridors managed for recreation, transportation, and conservation purposes. They can be as elaborate as a lengthy, paved hiking-biking-riding route or as simple, natural, and ecologically important as a stretch of stream bank left wild.

Greenways have multiple purposes, but from a recreation perspective they have two major functions:

1) To link and facilitate hike and bike access between residential areas and parks

2) To provide opportunities for the linear forms of outdoor recreation (e.g. hiking, jogging, bicycling, inline skating, horseback riding, cross-country skiing, and ordinary walking) in which many North Americans engage today. These recreation roles require the development of trails along the greenways.

Those instances in which a greenway is not a wide swath, but rather a narrow corridor in which a substantial portion of the corridor is occupied by a trail, are conceptually different from parklands and open space. Such greenways do not provide the extended tranquil views that underlie increases in proximate property values provided by parklands and open space. Instead, the enhanced property value associated with such greenways is likely to come from access to the trail and its functionality or activity potential.

The suggestion that access to narrow trails of this nature enhances property values is nearly always controversial. When the issue is debated in communities, much depends on public perceptions of who is likely to use the trail and for what purpose. For example, if the public perceives that the trail may facilitate the movement of economically disadvantaged residents through a relatively affluent neighborhood, the trail may be supported by the former and by the public at large but resisted by some people in the latter group who fear a decrease in their property values.

Relatively few empirical studies of the impact of trails on property values have been completed. Among the nine studies the author found addressing this issue were eight that relied on opinion surveys of homeowners, residents, developers, and realtors, and only one that used trends in market transactions (Crompton 2001b). The researchers assumed that these attitudes and opinions reflected residents' or homeowners' personal experiences, and the professional expertise of developers and realtors. These survey studies are less definitive and convincing than studies that examine trends in market transactions. Nevertheless, until this latter type of research is undertaken, such survey results represent the best available evidence.

The sample sizes in many of these studies were small, but the consistent pattern emerging from them and the diversity of environments and jurisdictions in which they were conducted made some general conclusions possible. Across the studies, for instance, there was broad consensus that trails have no negative impact on either the ability of owners to sell property or the value of the property. In these studies, between 20 percent and 40 percent of survey respondents believed that there was a positive impact on salability and value. The dominant prevailing sentiment, however, was that the presence of a trail had no impact on the ability to sell a property or on its value (Crompton 2001b).

For most people who reside adjacent or close to trails, the advantages of hike-and-bike access to other amenities and the opportunities that trails provide for linear outdoor recreation activities appear to be countered by the increased flow of people and reduced privacy that trails bring to a neighborhood. This suggests that the challenge for trail advocates is to design trails to alleviate these concerns.

Some potential buyers of a property may have no interest in hike/bike trails or linear recreation activities, so for them there is no positive counterbalance for the potential negative impacts of privacy loss, people flow, and noise. For other potential buyers, especially perhaps those with young children, hiking, biking, and linear recreation activities may be a central feature of their lifestyle, so access to trails far outweighs the perceived potential negative outcomes. These dichotomous lifestyles suggest why some are likely to respond positively to trails, while others remain more circumspect.

Across the studies . . . there was broad consensus that trails have no negative impact on either the ability of owners to sell property or the value of the property.

THE RELATIVE SERVICE COST EFFICIENCIES OF PARKS AND OPEN SPACE

The positions espoused in the sidebar on the facing page by the two sides debating the relative economic merits of using land for development or for parkland and open space are echoed in communities across the country. The conventional wisdom that prevails among many decision makers and taxpayers is that development is the "highest and best use" of vacant land for increasing municipal revenues. Developers who claim their projects "pay for themselves and then some" reinforce this conventional wisdom. They say that their projects will increase the municipal tax base and thereby lower each individual's property tax payments. This is the case in both growing communities and in built-out communities.

This belief resides deep in the American psyche and frequently has thwarted the conservation efforts of park and open space advocates. The reduction in financial aid from federal, state, and county governments and the ongoing resistance of residents to tax increases, in some cases, has made citizens and local officials even more receptive to such arguments.

The results of fiscal impact analyses and cost of community services (COCS) analyses, however, have shown that these beliefs, desires, and fears need to be reexamined. These analyses consistently report that over a wide range of residential densities, and especially in rapidly growing communities, the public costs associated with residential development exceed the public revenue that accrues from it. The traditional belief that development pays its way is being discarded. The emerging prevailing view is that few residential developments generate sufficient tax payments to pay their way (Crompton 2001c).

The people who reside in residential developments require services. Natural parks and open space require few public services—no roads, no

CONTROVERSY AT CITY HALL: OPEN SPACE OR DEVELOPMENT?

The gavel came down upon the desk with a loud, resonating thump that immediately brought silence to the small but crowded room. As the din of voices faded into a whisper and ceased altogether, the municipal clerk announced, "The meeting of the Hometown City Council will now come to order."

Hesitantly, because he could sense that the meeting would be long and tiresome, the mayor rose to address his fellow councilmen and the anxious crowd. "The purpose of tonight's meeting is to discuss the possible acquisition by this community of property known as the Scenic View Farm.

"As most of you know, this property consists of about 200 acres and includes open fields, woods, a stream, and an overlook from which the whole community can be viewed. I realize that the potential acquisition is controversial; therefore, all those who desire to speak will be given an opportunity to be heard."

Immediately a hand rose in the audience. At a gesture from the mayor, a woman rose and stated, "My name is Pauline Smedley. I live on Anderson Road and I am representing the Hometown Citizens Taxpayers Association. We are opposed to the acquisition of the Scenic View Farm and feel that its acquisition with public funds would not be in the best interest of the community's residents.

"Already our property taxes are unbearable. This acquisition would result in a tax increase since the property would be removed from the tax rolls. On the other hand, if the tract were developed, more homes would produce more tax revenues, which would result in keeping our tax rate from increasing. This community, in all good conscience, cannot afford to allow potential taxable property from being constructed. We hope that the council will, in the best interests of the community, vote not to acquire the property." As she sat down members of the taxpayers association applauded loudly.

"Your Honor," a voice from the other side of the room called out. "I'd like to present an opposing viewpoint."

"Please proceed," responded the mayor.

"My name is Joe Tucker," the second speaker said. "I represent the Citizens for a Quality Environment of Hometown, and we fully support the Scenic View Farm acquisition. In our rapidly growing community, the few remaining open spaces should be preserved, not only for scenic and environmental reasons, which are important, but also because it's good business.

"It's not true that more development is the answer to our rising tax rate; in fact, it is often the cause of it. If the farm were to be developed, it would cost the community more to provide services to the development than the community would receive in tax revenues. This deficit would have to be made up by increasing the tax rate.

"Open space, however, doesn't demand municipal services. It costs the community little beyond acquisition expenses but provides many economic benefits. In fact, the projected deficit created by the cost of servicing the development exceeding the taxes received from it would be adequate in seven years to pay for the farm's acquisition as open space. Open space keeps our taxes low, and we urge the council to act in the best interests of the community by acquiring the property."

Having heard diametrically opposed arguments, the council postponed making its decision until its members had sufficient information to fully evaluate the economic aspects of the proposed acquisition. ■

Source: Adapted from Caputo (1979)

schools, no sewage, no solid waste disposal, no water, and minimal fire and police protection. Thus, park and open space land often is less costly for public agencies to maintain and operate than residential property. This is a long-term benefit of preserving open space not usually reflected in market valuations of land because valuations generally reflect only the short-term benefit of land.

In the mid-1980s, the American Farmland Trust developed a relatively inexpensive procedure for assessing the costs and revenues of community services associated with different land uses, which included open space. The broad categories of land used in these evaluations are: residential development, commercial/industrial development, and farmland/forestland/open space (Miller 1992).

A summary of results from COCS analyses done in 58 communities, in 18 different states, by 26 different research teams is given in Figure 2.5 (Crompton 2001c). The main commonality among the studies is that most of the selected communities were relatively small and incorporated farmland in their tax base.

FIGURE 2-5. The median cost, per dollar revnue raised, to provide public services to different land uses (n=58 communities).

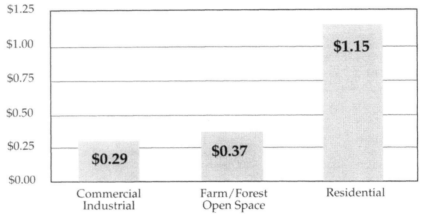

Source: American Farmland Trust, Farmland Information Center, Technical Assistance Division, Northampton, MA.

Figure 2-5 shows the median cost per dollar of revenue raised to provide public services to each of the three different land uses among the 58 communities analyzed. Thus, for every $1 million in tax revenues these communities received from farm/forest/open space uses and from industrial/commercial uses, the median amount they had to expend to provide them with public services was only $370,000 and $290,000, respectively. In contrast, for every $1 million received in revenues from residential developments, the median amount the communities had to expend to service them was $1,150,000. The results of these studies indicate that favoring residential development at the expense of open land does not alleviate the financial problems of communities. Indeed, it is likely to exacerbate them.

The data from these empirical studies group publicly owned parks and open space with privately owned agricultural land, forestland, and vacant lots. However, the revenue implications associated with this undeveloped land are quite different in the public and private sectors. Revenues accruing to the city from publicly owned land are likely to be minimal—limited to net receipts from admission fees, concessions, grazing rights, or lease income from tenant farmers. In contrast, even if the private lands are protected by conservation easements and taxed at their use or productive value rather than appraised value so property taxes are low, they still yield some tax revenue to the community.

Residential development is the most common alternate use proposed for potential park and open space lands. Thus, because only nominal revenue is likely to accrue from public park and open space lands, the key fiscal impact question becomes: Will the net costs of purchasing, maintaining, and operating the land as a park or as open space be greater than the net costs associated with servicing a residential development that may be constructed on that site? Evidence discussed earlier in this chapter suggests that the purchase cost is likely to be paid for by increases in proximate property values. Hence, the fiscal impact comparison involves only the park or open space land's maintenance and operating expenses.

The sidebar to the right uses the same nature-oriented park site described in the beginning of this chapter (Figure 2-1) and the data summarized in Figure 2-5 to illustrate how to undertake the comparative fiscal impact analysis. In the context provided, the illustration suggests that if the annual cost of maintaining and operating the natural park is less than $112,500, it is likely to be less of a financial burden to the community than a residential development on the 50-acre site.

Furthermore, investment in parks and open space does not incur the externality costs that accompany residential development—traffic congestion, noise, crime, pollution, infrastructure deterioration, and changes in community character. The COCS methodology does not include quantification of the costs of these externalities, but presumably they add to the appeal of using land for open space rather than developing it.

FISCAL ANALYSIS OF THE RELATIVE IMPACT FOR ALTERNATIVE LAND USES OF A 720-ACRE FARM IN MANSFIELD TOWNSHIP, NEW JERSEY

When a 720-acre farm property became available for sale, the Mansfield Township's zoning ordinance would have permitted 300 units of small, clustered housing to be developed on the site. The average cost per household to the school district, assuming one student per home, was $5,568. The average residential property tax, excluding county taxes, was $2,172. Given these data, the Township concluded:

a) The annual cost to the school district would be approximately $1,670,400 ($5,568 x 300 children).

b) The anticipated revenue would be approximately $651,600 ($2,172 x 300 homes).

c) The annual deficit for the school district budget would be $1,018,800 ($1,670,400 – $651,600).

The cost of purchasing the development rights of the 720-acre farm was $10.4 million. The public investment for the development rights could be offset in less than 15 years by avoiding the higher costs associated with development of the farm. From then on, the town would receive only the positive revenue flow from the farmland and attain the statewide and municipal goal of farmland preservation. In contrast, the cost of services for a residential development would continue forever. ■

Source: Adapted Association of New Jersey Environmental Commissions (1996).

AN ILLUSTRATIVE COMPARISON OF THE NET COST OF SERVING A RESIDENTIAL DEVELOPMENT AND A NATURAL PARK AREA

On the 50-acre site (Figure 2-1), assume a density of three homes per acre and a property tax rate (school district, city, county et al.) of 2.5 percent of market value on these $200,000 homes. Thus, annual property tax revenue equals $750,000 (50 x 3 x $5,000).

Assume that the cost of servicing these residences is 15 percent higher than the property taxes received (Figure 2-5). Thus, the annual net loss to the community for servicing this residential development is $112,500 ([(115 ÷ 100) x $750,000] – $750,000).

If the operation and maintenance cost of the 50-acre natural park is lower than $112,500 per year, it is a less expensive option to service than the housing development on the same site. ■

THE PITTSFORD SOLUTION

In 1998, the American Planning Association recognized the innovative conservation action taken by the Town of Pittsford, New York, located seven miles southeast of Rochester, by awarding the town its annual Current Topic Award. Land development in Pittsford was consuming important agricultural landscapes, scenic vistas, and other natural and cultural resources. A comprehensive planning process, involving more than 100 public meetings, workshops, and focus groups sessions, resulted in a community consensus for the preservation of these central features of the town's character. The outcome was development of a precedent-setting plan for permanently protecting its greenspaces that the American Planning Association considered to be "exemplary."

A key element in their decision process was the results of a fiscal impact analysis that predicted future tax rates based upon the costs and revenues associated with future land-use patterns. The fiscal impact analysis revealed the following:

- If the town did nothing, the typical household would pay increased taxes of several hundred dollars per year to support growth.

- The break-even value of a new home was more than $300,000. Break-even occurs when the tax revenue gained from the addition of a house equals the cost of community services attributable to a new home.

- Increased commercial development could decrease future tax increases.

- The break-even cost for the town to purchase development rights on farms and other open space resources in the path of development was about $10,000 per acre. The break-even cost occurs when the cost of financing a bond to purchase the development rights for an acre equals the additional cost to the community of developing an acre for residential use.

The fiscal impact analysis demonstrated that it would be less expensive to implement a revised land-use plan than to follow the current zoning policies. The revised plan included purchase of conservation easements on important farmland and open space resources, coupled with a policy of creating several enhanced economic development sites for commercial and light industrial business expansion.

The fiscal impact analysis showed that protection of open space, including purchase of development rights, would cost taxpayers less per year for support of community services than full build-out of the town.

This finding did not mean that there should be no further development. It meant that a fiscal balance could be achieved through a strategy that promoted a variety of housing types, recognized the need for the development of economic land uses, and preserved open space. Using the fiscal model as a planning tool, the targets for land preservation and development were tested, modified, and refined.

The plan protected more than 2,000 acres, which represented about two-thirds of the remaining undeveloped land in the town. Three mechanisms were used:

- Purchase of development rights on 1,200 acres

- Incentive zoning (transfer of development rights) on 200-plus acres

- Mandatory clustering protecting 600-plus acres.

The purchase of development rights program protecting 1,200 acres was directed at seven farms. The average cost to a homeowner of the purchases was approximately $50 per year. In contrast, the fiscal impacts analysis estimated that homeowners would face an average tax increase of $250 per year if the development rights program was not implemented and a projected 1,000 plus new homes were built on this land. Avoiding these tax costs saved the average homeowner about $5,000 over the life of the bonds issued to purchase the development rights that were acquired at an average price of $9,000 per acre. *Source: Behan (1999)*

These kinds of analyses have caused some communities to consider purchasing land or development rights rather than incur the losses likely to accrue from development. Examples of this are described in the Mansfield Township sidebar at the bottom of page 23 and the Pittsford sidebar on page 24.

Bucknall (1989, 9) has suggested that communities striving to reduce the tax burdens on citizens may not fully appreciate the increase in the scope and level of services that will have to be provided to different categories of land use. The costs and benefits of parks and open space have largely been ignored by fiscal impact studies in the past. Results from COCS studies undertaken in the past 15 years provide evidence of the need to include parks and open space in the fiscal and economic discourse.

The intent in this section is not to suggest that one type of development is a superior land use to another because some combination of all three land uses (residential, commercial/industrial, and open space) is needed in viable communities. Rather, the intent is to point out that using land for parks and open space is relevant to discussions concerned with enhancing a community's fiscal health. The goal is not to prevent growth, but to encourage a balance between development and open space

USING THE PLANNING TOOLKIT WITH THE PROXIMATE PRINCIPLE
Planners have sometimes activated the proximate principle to create vehicles that directly capture the incremental gains to property values and used them to pay for park acquisition and development costs by retaining the increments in a separate account for that purpose instead of returning them to the general fund. Four of these vehicles are excess condemnation, special assessment districts, tax increment financing districts, and exaction accounts.

Excess Purchase/Condemnation
The excess/purchase condemnation principle involves purchasing more land than is needed for the park project; developing the park, thus appreciating the value of the remaining land; disposing of the remainder on a commercial basis; and applying the income derived to pay for the original investment. In short, the governmental jurisdiction acts in a role similar to that of a developer. Some agencies may lack the enabling legislative authority to do this and private developers are likely to strenuously oppose any action of this type. Nevertheless, the example in the sidebar illustrates how it could work (Cook 1994).

Where there is no legal authority for a public agency to use this strategy, or where elected officials are unwilling to face the controversy such an action would generate, nonprofit agencies often fill the void. They can purchase tracts of land that include sections desired by agencies for parks or open space. After conveying these sections, they can resell the remaining land to developers using profits to finance the total transaction.

A variation of the excess purchase principle is emerging in golf residential developments where some developers now donate land to a municipality for a golf course, while retaining the property around it. The land donation is paid for by the increased property value the course creates, while the developer receives a tax write-off for the donation and avoids the costs associated with constructing a course and subsequently owning and managing it (Winton 1994, Crossley 1986, Marchant 1995).

Special Assessment Districts
The lively controversy that invariably accompanies excess purchase led others to suggest that special assessments offered a more feasible method of

THE BURLINGTON, VERMONT, WATERFRONT PARK SYSTEM AND URBAN RESERVE

Burlington, Vermont, purchased a 20-acre property that, when developed as parkland (at the time of purchase it was a tank farm), would complete its Lake Champlain waterfront park system. This park system was seen as a primary catalyst in the city's future economic development. The city also purchased an adjoining 25-acre property that it planned to hold as an "urban reserve" for which a future generation of Burlington citizens would determine appropriate development, probably a combination of residential and commercial. This property was purchased with city pension fund money. The idea was that the property would appreciate dramatically in value as the new waterfront park was fully developed (the tank farm had a five-year lease). This purchase exemplified a long-term vision of how parks could stimulate surrounding property values and new investment.

securing the enhancement increment. The city of Minneapolis has one of the finest park systems in the country. That system was developed primarily through the use of special assessments. When the city was growing rapidly in the first half of the twentieth century, there was a belief that improvements should not be paid for by the city as a whole, but by special assessments levied solely against the properties that benefited. The Elwell law passed by the state legislature in 1911 provided the enabling legislation to accomplish the following.

In a typical case, a new park costing $3,000,000 would be planned to serve one square mile of the city containing 3,000 lots, all within 5 or 6 blocks of the site. The average assessment in such a case would be $1,000 per lot, payable at $50 a year for 20 years, plus 5 percent interest. Lots nearest the park may have to pay as much as $75 per year while those five blocks away may pay $25 a year (Brecher and Brecher 1963, 479).

This graduated system of park taxes in which the highest taxes were paid by properties closest to the park was practical public recognition of the enhanced value that parks provide. Kansas City and Denver also used special assessment districts to develop park systems in their formative years.

Special assessments do not work well, however, in areas where the cost of land is high and the surrounding homes are poor. This, in fact, is the reason that Minneapolis abandoned the special assessment strategy in the 1960s. There was concern that heavy reliance on special assessment districts was creating a two-tier system of parks (Martin 1994). Hence, Minneapolis scrapped this system and reverted to a citywide charge on each property, dedicating the revenue from that charge for park development.

Nevertheless, there are many contemporary examples where special assessment districts have been used to finance parks that convey benefits only to those in a selected geographical area. In some enabling legislation, special assessment districts are also termed enhancement districts, benefit assessment districts, improvement park districts, special services districts, or business improvement districts. Local governments form them because most property owners within the district's boundaries want a higher level of service than the standard that the city provides. Hence, the property owners agree to assess themselves an additional property or sales tax to pay for this higher level of service. The tax is apportioned according to a formula designed to reflect the proportion of benefits that accrue to each property owner. For example, people whose property is located on the fringe of the district may be assessed less than people whose property abuts the park or facility. The special assessment district tax is identified separately on tax bills.

Where the higher level of service that taxpayers desire refers to acquisition and development of new facilities, rather than to higher standards of operation and maintenance, special assessment bonds may be issued to finance the capital improvements. Because the benefit is confined to a carefully defined area of the community, only those people who will benefit from the improvement bear the cost. The director of parks and recreation in New York City observed, "It's like upgrading an airline ticket to first-class" (Martin 1994, p. A16).

Where business leaders initiate special assessment districts, areas benefiting from the special assessment are called business improvement districts (BIDs). There are more than 1,000 BIDs in the United States and Canada. These districts often elect their own boards, which take responsibility for the annual budget, hire staff, let contracts, and generally oversee operations. Much of their effort goes into cleaning up, landscaping, maintaining trees and flowers, and enhancing security. Bryant Park, one of the country's great park success stories, is the result of a BID. The sidebar very briefly describes how the BID worked. (Also see Garvin 2000, 44-45.)

Megan Lewis

USING A BUSINESS IMPROVEMENT DISTRICT TO RESUSCITATE BRYANT PARK

Bryant Park, which sits beside the New York Public Library, was a neglected, vandalized facility that by the late 1970s had become a haven for drug dealers. A business improvement district (BID) was formed to maintain the nine-acre park and make ongoing park improvements. The park has been restored with tall shade trees, lush green grass, flower beds, pagodas, and a thriving restaurant, and is now considered a model park. At its summer peak, there are 55 employees working in Bryant Park in security, sanitation, gardening, and special events. All of them work for the BID. On some days, the park attracts more than 4,000 office workers and tourists, and more than 10,000 people attend some special events.

Mary Eysenbach

The city paid one-third of the $18 million restoration costs, and foundations, philanthropists, and surrounding businesses financed the rest through the BID. The businesses assess themselves $1.2 million of Bryant Park's $2 million annual maintenance bill, while the remainder of the bill is raised in rental and concession fees from restaurants and special events held in the park.

Businesses recognized that property values and hence, lease rentals, were closely tied to conditions in the park. Rents in nearby buildings increased dramatically after the park was redesigned and secured. To a primary organizer of the Bryant Park effort, the lesson was clear: "If building owners and the agents help protect urban open space they will be more than paid back for their efforts, both in increased occupancy rates and in increased rent—all because their building has this attractive new front yard."

Source: Lerner and Poole (1999)

Tax Increment Financing

A majority of states have enabling legislation authorizing a now well-known and widely used planning tool—tax increment financing (TIF). (See PAS Report No. 389 for a more detailed description of how TIF works. We will provide only a brief description here.) The initial task is to designate an area as a TIF district. The local development authority or city then issues tax increment bonds and uses the proceeds to acquire land and to develop parks, open space, infrastructure, or other public improvements in the district.

Tax increment bonds are secured only by projected increases in revenues from existing and new development in the tax increment financing district. Repayment is contingent upon increases in the taxable value of the property in the district. The distinctive feature of tax increment financing districts is that they rely on property taxes that the projects within the district directly create. The projects, not the general taxpayers, pay for redevelopment costs. Because rejuvenation of the district is likely to increase the value of their assets, landowners and residents have every reason to support the district's establishment.

Exactions

A final application of the proximate principle that planners may wish to consider is a suggestion for using it to rectify a weakness of exaction ordinances. Most communities have passed ordinances that embrace the principle that neighborhood parks should be financed by development in the neighborhood because development creates the demand for parks. The ordinances typically require developers to provide land or fees in lieu of land dedication. In most cases, communities opt to take the fees-in-lieu because either the amount of land required to be dedicated is too small for practical use as a park, or it is not of the quality desired.

When sufficient fees-in-lieu have been collected, the community seeks to buy a neighborhood park with those fees. Unfortunately, by the time sufficient funds have been collected, appropriate land for a neighborhood park in the area is frequently not available because it has all been developed. To avoid this situation, an alternative would be for the community to buy neighborhood parks in advance of development, using the principle pioneered by Olmsted in the 1850s, and finance them by subsequent exaction fees and the increased value in properties around them. The sidebar describes a proposal being considered by College Station, Texas, that embraces this approach.

USING THE PROXIMATE PRINCIPLE AND CERTIFICATES OF OBLIGATION TO DEVELOP GOOD NEIGHBORHOOD PARKS IN COLLEGE STATION, TEXAS

Through its revision of the parks dedication ordinance in 1999, the College Station, Texas, City Council established the principle that neighborhood parks should be financed by development in the neighborhood because development creates the demand for parks.

The ordinance requires that developers dedicate an acre of land per 100 single homes (or per 134 multifamily units). The council wanted to make parks neighborhood focal points and to expand their use to include a broader range of intergenerational activities with more passive park areas, so the Parks Board recommended the standard size for neighborhood parks be changed from 5 to 15 acres to 12 to 15 acres.

The difficulty in meeting that standard was twofold. First, most developments in the city are too small to generate the amount of land to meet the standard. Consequently, the city frequently accepts the alternative dedication of cash in lieu of the land from developers. When sufficient cash accrues from these payments, the city would attempt to purchase adequate land for a neighborhood park. The second problem was that by the time enough money was paid in lieu of land dedication, the land most suited for a neighborhood park of appropriate size had been acquired for development. Invariably, the only land available for a neighborhood park is floodplain or retention pond land that developers cannot use, but which is also often inferior for use as a neighborhood park.

To illustrate this problem, the College Station Parks Board and the Planning and Zoning Commission provided the council a table showing (below) the composition of the neighborhood parks approved since 1996.

	Westfield	Bella Vista	Steeplechase	Shenandoah	Woodland Hills	Edelweiss
Total acres	3.44	7.7428	9.09	8.26	13.91	11.01
Floodplain	1.71	0	5.66	0	6.4l	0
Detention	0	N/A	1.18	5.68	.95	6.70
Floodplain and detention	1.71	N/A	6.84	5.68	7.42	6.70
Remaining area	1.73	N/A	2.25	2.58	6.49	4.31

To solve the problem, the board and commission recommended a program in which the city issues Certificates of Obligation to purchase neighborhood park sites of 12 to15 acres in advance of development. At $10,000 an acre, this would involve a commitment of $120,000 to $150,000 per park. These purchases would be made five to seven years in advance of projected development, using a similar timeframe to that used by the school district. The certificates would be repaid over time from two sources: (1) by the cash in lieu payments that the dedication ordinance requires developers to contribute for neighborhood parks; and (2) by the enhanced property taxes the city will obtain from residences in close proximity to these parks as a result of the presence of the parks.

CHAPTER 3

Attracting Tourists

The broad field of travel is commonly divided into four major segments based upon the purpose of the trip:

1) business-related travel;

2) personal business, including visiting friends or relatives;

3) conventions and meetings; and

4) pleasure travel.

There is some overlap between these trip purpose segments. For example, while the primary purpose of a trip may be attending a convention or visiting friends and relatives, the trip may also turn into pleasure travel.

Traditionally, the term "tourist" referred only to pleasure travelers and did not embrace the other three trip purposes. The inclination of most public tourism agencies and private tourism advocacy groups today is to extend the definition of tourism to include all these segments because the broader tourism is defined, the more visitors it embraces and the larger its economic value is perceived to be. This is a psychological repositioning strategy that leads to enhancement of the stature and visibility of those in a community associated with tourism, enabling them to position themselves more favorably in the psyche of both the general public and legislators.

The broader tourism is defined, the more visitors it embraces and the larger its economic value is perceived to be.

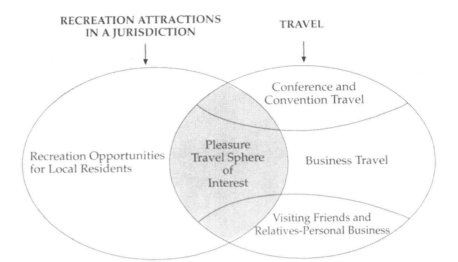

FIGURE 3-1. Segments of travel and their interrelationship

Tourism agencies are unlikely to have any influence on business travel or on visiting friends and relatives. The two segments of travel that are most likely to be responsive to their efforts are conference and convention travel and pleasure travel. The shaded area in Figure 3-1 indicates that this latter segment is a primary sphere of interest and influence for those responsible for parks and recreation management and activities. When recreation attractions are perceived to be the primary purpose of travel, park advocates often can claim that parks and recreation are the primary engines that drive tourism's economic impact in a community.

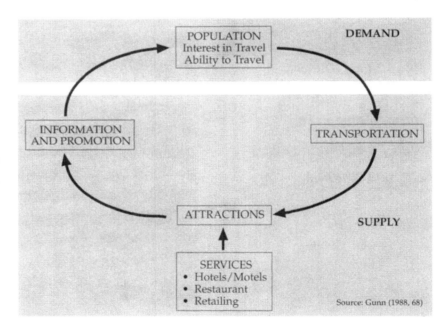

FIGURE 3-2. A simplified model of a tourism system.

Figure 3-2 shows a simplified model of a tourism system (Gunn 1988). It indicates that visitors use some mode of transportation (e.g., automobile or airplane) to leave their homes and travel to attractions, which are supported by various kinds of services (e.g., hotels/motels, restaurants, retailing). The attractions and support services provide information and promote their offerings to target groups they have identified as potential visitors.

This tourism system is activated by attractions. Only in rare cases do people leave their home and travel some distance by automobile, airplane, or ship because they want to stay in a particular hotel or dine at a particular restaurant in a different locale. Most of the time, the desire to go to a destination on a pleasure trip is stimulated by its attractions.

A taxonomy of attractions likely to activate pleasure travel is shown in the sidebar at the right. Perusal of this list of tourist attractions leads to the conclusion that almost all of them are developed by, and in most cases are operated by, the public sector or by nonprofit organizations. This leads to the conclusion that, *in most communities, pleasure travel is a business that the public sector drives, and agencies responsible for park and recreation amenities and events are central to that business, which, in turn, are really the engines of tourism.* For example, the sidebar below lists the potential tourist attractions in the city of Baton Rouge, Louisiana. All of them are operated by public or nonprofit organizations.

BATON ROUGE, LOUISIANA, ATTRACTIONS

Zoo

Arboretum-Botanical Garden

Horse Activities Enter

Highland Observatory

Magnolia Mound Historical Home

Olympia Field (High School)

Six Public Golf Courses

Softball/Baseball Fields

Frisbee Golf Courses

Velodrome

BMX Track

Six Public Tennis Centers

Old State Capitol

State Capitol

Old Governor's Mansion Museum

Arts and Science Center, Centroplex

Rural Life Museum, Hope Plantation

Louisiana State University, Tiger Football Stadium and John Parker Agricultural Center

Pete Marovich Assembly Center

Southern University Stadium

A TAXONOMY OF TOURIST ATTRACTIONS

Arts
Theaters
Art Galleries
Museums
Performing groups, Music concerts

Heritage Places
Ethnic cultural places
Shrines/churches
Historical sites and structures
Educational institutions
Industry factory tours

Parks
National
State
Regional
Local
Beaches
Theme parks

Recreation
Events and festivals
Aquatic and coastal areas
Outdoor recreations (e.g., camping, fishing, hunting)
Sports (e.g., golf, tennis, skiing, sailing, softball)
Fitness and wellness centers

Arenas
College sports
Professional franchises
Concerts and exhibitions

Other
Gambling places
Cruise ships

This central role in tourism is not part of the position that most park advocate agencies and organizations currently occupy in stakeholders' minds. Indeed, it is the antithesis of the general public's and tourism field's conventional wisdom. Most people are under the misapprehension that tourism is the almost exclusive preserve of the commercial sector. The commercial sector offers essential transportation; support services, such as accommodations, restaurants, and retailing; and information and promotion

Public park and recreation agencies traditionally have provided financial reports, whereas tourism organizations have learned to provide economic reports.

dissemination (see Figure 3-2). In most communities, however, the public sector is the primary provider of the attractions that activate pleasure travel.

Very few communities have large-scale commercial tourist attractions. Despite their absence, most jurisdictions recognize the importance of tourism to economic development and establish convention and visitor bureaus or similar agencies, whose primary mission is to attract visitors. They invariably rely on the park and recreation agency to create attractions that will persuade visitors to come to the community and spend money there.

The extent to which the planning department, the park and recreation agency, and Friends of the Parks groups constitute the engine of tourism in any particular community can be ascertained by listing all the programs, festivals, tournaments, competitions, and facilities operated or co-sponsored by those groups that attract pleasure travelers to the community from out of town, such as was done in Baton Rouge. To provide contrast, a list of commercial attractions should be prepared. In most communities, the commercial attractions list will be the shortest. In such cases, this competitive repositioning strategy will show the relative insignificance of commercial enterprises in attracting visitors to the community when compared to the public sector attractions. The dissemination of such comparative lists may make an effective contribution to repositioning parks and recreation as being central to tourism in the minds of stakeholders.

THE ROLE OF ECONOMIC IMPACT STUDIES

To demonstrate their economic contributions and the centrality of their role to a community's tourism efforts, the agencies and organizations responsible for parks and recreation must undertake economic impact studies. When the parks and recreation department in city A reported the financial consequences of hosting a national softball championship tournament, it reported a loss of $9,375. When the convention and visitors bureau in that community reported the consequences of hosting the same event, it reported an economic gain to the community of $525,000. It is obvious which agency was likely to be viewed most positively by elected officials and taxpayers!

Why did two agencies report such disparate data from the same event? The answer to this question is that they used different approaches for demonstrating accountability for their public funds.

Public park and recreation agencies traditionally have provided financial reports, whereas tourism organizations have learned to provide economic reports. The different reporting methods have resulted in the two types of agencies occupying very different positions in the minds of public officials. By using economic reports, many convention and visitor bureaus have persuaded elected officials and decision makers that they are central contributors to their communities' economic health. In contrast, park and recreation agencies generally have not been successful in creating a similar central position in decision makers' minds regarding the economic contribution of their services because they have used only financial reports.

Hence, in a climate of fiscal conservatism, public agencies whose activities are related to parks, open space, and recreation are mistakenly perceived to be "black hats" whose services result in net economic losses to the community, while convention and visitor bureaus have established themselves as "white hats" because they bring new money into the community.

Figure 3-3 illustrates the conceptual reasoning for developing economic balance sheets to supplement financial information. It shows that residents

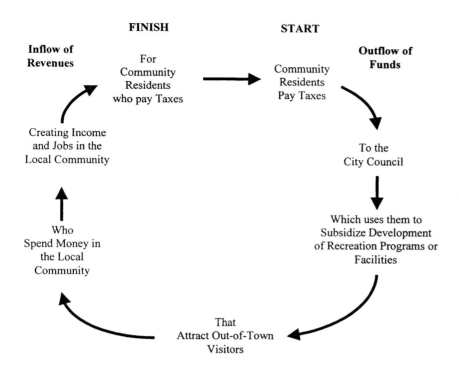

FINISH   **START**

Inflow of Revenues

For Community Residents who pay Taxes

Creating Income and Jobs in the Local Community

Who Spend Money in the Local Community

Community Residents Pay Taxes

Outflow of Funds

To the City Council

Which uses them to Subsidize Development of Recreation Programs or Facilities

That Attract Out-of-Town Visitors

FIGURE 3-3. The conceptual rational for developing an economic balance sheet.

of a community "give" funds to their city council in the form of taxes. The city council uses a proportion of these funds to subsidize production of an event or development of a facility. The facility or event attracts nonresident visitors who spend money in the local community both inside and outside of the events and facilities that they visit. This new money from outside of the community creates income and jobs in the community for residents. This completes the virtuous cycle of economic development. Community residents are responsible for providing the initial funds, and they receive a return on their investment in the form of new jobs and more household income.

Agencies and organizations that assist in the development of park and recreation facilities in a community essentially provide seed money and in-kind resources to leverage substantial economic gains for the community. If public sector resources are not used to financially underwrite the cost of staging these events, the consequent economic benefits to the local community will not accrue. Private enterprises are unlikely to commit funds to organizing such events because they are unable to capture a large enough proportion of the income spent by participants to obtain a satisfactory return on their investment.

The traditional financial balance sheet presented by many public agencies assumes that the cycle shown in Figure 3-3 starts and ends with the city council rather than with a community's residents. This is narrow and misleading because it includes only the taxes and revenues that accrue to local government from the event or facility. Such a narrow definition suggests that concern should be focused on income accruing to the council from lease fees, admission revenues, increased sales tax revenues, and other revenue sources. This approach, however, is flawed conceptually because the money invested does not belong to the council; rather, it belongs to the city's residents. Although it is efficient for the residents' investment to be funneled through the council, the return that *residents* receive is what is important, not merely the proportion of the total return that filters back to the council. The purpose of economic impact studies is to measure the economic return to residents.

Although it is efficient for the residents' investment to be funneled through the council, the return that residents receive is what is important, not merely the proportion of the total return that filters back to the council.

**A COMPARISON OF THE ECONOMIC RETURN AND
THE FINANCIAL RETURN**
City A's Amateur Softball Association's Men's 40-and-Over
Fast-Pitch National Tournament

Context

All 37 teams that qualified for the tournament were from outside the local area. The average number of players per team was 15. Some players brought family and friends with them, so the average size of the contingent associated with each team, including the players, was 21. Because it was an elimination tournament, the length of time that the teams stayed in the community varied from two to six nights.

Economic Return

A survey of the players revealed the following:

- Total expenditures in the local area by players and their family and friends: $287,000

- An input-output model that calculated multipliers concluded the following:

  Total economic impact on sales: $525,000

  Total economic impact on personal income: $164,000

Financial Return

- Income to the city parks and recreation department from entry fees: $4,625
- Costs incurred by the department, including manpower, to host the event: $14,000
- Net financial loss to the city: $9,375

Pay-Back Period

The cost of constructing the softball complex was almost $2 million. Based on economic return to residents in terms of personal income, the capital cost of the complex would be repaid after 14 similar tournaments.

The difference between the financial and economic approaches is illustrated in the above sidebar. The financial balance sheet shows a net loss of $9,375 from a tournament. However, on the economic balance sheet, a net return of $273,000, $511,000, or $150,000 is the result, depending on whether economic impact was reported in terms of direct expenditures, sales impact, or impact on personal incomes. (These figures were calculated by taking the gross amounts shown and subtracting from them the $14,000 costs incurred by the department to host the event.)

The capital cost of the softball complex was approximately $2 million, which means that if the personal income measure of economic impact were used (the reasons for preferring this measure are discussed in the next section of the chapter), the investment would pay for itself after 14 similar tournaments.

How many other investments is a jurisdiction likely to have that pay for themselves in two years (assuming seven tournaments per year) and that continue to contribute $1 million to residents annually for the next 20 years? Agencies and organizations that can present these kind of data in the form of an economic balance sheet to their stakeholders, demonstrating their contribution to economic development, are likely to reposition themselves favorably in the minds of legislators and the general public.

THE BASIC PRINCIPLES OF ECONOMIC IMPACT STUDIES

A detailed description on how to undertake economic impact studies is available elsewhere (Crompton 1999) and is beyond the scope of this publication, but a brief review of the principles involved is needed in order to interpret the results of studies presented in the next section of this chapter.

Economic impact analysis is an inexact process, and output numbers should be regarded as a best guess rather than as being inviolably accurate. Indeed, if five different individuals undertook a study, it is probable that there would be five different results. Most research projects are predicated on a search for truth, but, unfortunately, the goal in economic impact studies often is less auspicious; it is to legitimize a position. Usually they are undertaken in order to justify a public expenditure in quantitative dollar terms, with the expectation that the results will reinforce the case for sustaining or increasing resources allocated to the service. In these circumstances, there is a temptation to manipulate the procedures to strengthen the case.

Most research projects are predicated on a search for truth, but, unfortunately, the goal in economic impact studies often is less auspicious; it is to legitimize a position.

There are several points in an analysis where underlying assumptions can be made that will substantially affect the final result. Unfortunately, this means there is a temptation to adopt inappropriate procedures and assumptions in order to generate high economic impact numbers that will position an agency more favorably in the minds of elected officials. Sometimes such errors are the result of a genuine lack of understanding of economic impact analysis and the procedures used in it, but in other instances they are committed deliberately and mischievously to generate large numbers and mislead stakeholders.

In this section, four principles central to the integrity of economic impact analyses are briefly reviewed:

1) exclusion of local residents;

2) exclusion of "time-switchers" and "casuals";

3) use of income rather than sales output measures of economic impact; and

4) careful interpretation of employment measures.

Mischievous manipulation of analyses invariably involves abusing one or more of these four principles.

Exclusion of Local Residents

Economic impact attributable to a recreation or park facility or event relates only to new money injected into an economy by visitors, media, vendors, external government entities, or banks and investors from outside the community. Only those visitors who reside outside the jurisdiction and whose primary motivation for visiting is to attend the facility or event, or who stay longer and spend more because of it, should be included in an economic impact study.

Expenditures by those who reside in the community do not contribute to a facility's economic impact because these expenditures represent a recycling of money. It is probable that if local residents had not spent this money at the facility, they would have disposed of it either now or later by purchasing other goods and services in the community. Twenty dollars spent by a local family at a community parks' event is likely to be 20 fewer dollars spent on movie tickets or other entertainment elsewhere in the community. Thus, expenditures associated with the facility by local residents are likely merely to be switched spending that offers no net economic stimulus to the community. Hence, it should not be included when estimating economic impact.

This widespread admonition from economists to disregard locals' expenditures is frequently ignored because when expenditures by local residents are omitted, the economic impact numbers become too small to be politically useful. To rectify this, two disconcerting new terms have emerged. Some tourism and economic development agencies now report that their facility contributed $X million "to local economic activity." Along with "economic activity," a synonymous term, "economic surge," is now being used. Both of these terms are used to describe *all* expenditures associated with an event or facility, irrespective of whether they derive from residents or from out-of-town visitors. This generates the high numbers that study sponsors invariably seek, but the economic surge or economic activity figures are meaningless. They are used by advocates to deliberately mislead stakeholders for the purpose of boosting their advocacy position. Unfortunately, this unethical strategy often succeeds because most elected officials, media representatives, and residents mistakenly assume that "economic activity" and "economic surge" are synonymous with measures of economic impact.

Exclusion of "Time-Switchers" and "Casuals"

Expenditures from out-of-town visitors should not include dollars spent by "time-switchers" and "casuals." For example, some nonlocal spectators at an event may have been planning a visit to the community for some time but changed the timing of their visit to coincide with the event. The spending in the community of these *time-switchers* cannot be attributed to the event since it would have occurred without the event, albeit at a different time of the year.

Casuals are visitors who were already in the community because they were attracted by other features and who elected to go to the event instead of doing something else. For example, in a survey of the economic impact of the Chicago Cubs' spring training on Mesa, Arizona, many respondents reported they were out-of-state residents (Howard and Crompton 1995). However, the Mesa area is a prime location for "snowbirds." Large numbers of these retired people lock up their homes in the Midwest for the four or five coldest winter months and migrate south to spend the winter in the warmth of Arizona. When respondents were asked if their decision to visit Mesa would be affected by a relocation of the Chicago Cubs to another state, approximately half of the out-of-state respondents indicated it would have no effect. Thus, the expenditures of these "casuals" could not be attributed to spring training because they were already in Mesa, and it is likely they would have spent that money in the community on something else if there had been no spring training.

Use of Income Rather than Sales Output Measures

Economic impact can be expressed by a variety of different indicators, but almost all of them involve use of the multiplier concept. Hence, the notion of multipliers is explained before the discussion shifts to the relative merit of using income or sales measures of economic impact.

The multiplier concept. The multiplier concept recognizes that when visitors to an event spend money in a community, their initial direct expenditure stimulates economic activity and creates additional business turnover, personal income, employment, and government revenue in the host community. The concept is based on recognition that the industries constituting an economy are interdependent; that is, each business will purchase goods and services produced by other establishments within the local economy. Thus, expenditures by visitors from outside the local economy will not only affect the business at which the initial expenditure is made, but also that business's suppliers, the suppliers' suppliers, and so on.

The impact of an injection of outside money by visitors can be likened to the ripples that occur in a pool if more water is poured into the system. The pool represents the economy, and the additional water symbolizes extra spending by the outside visitors. The ripples show the spread of money through the economy. Some of the money spent by visitors, however, leaks out of the city's economic system either to pay salaries or taxes to people or entities located outside the city, or to buy goods and services from them.

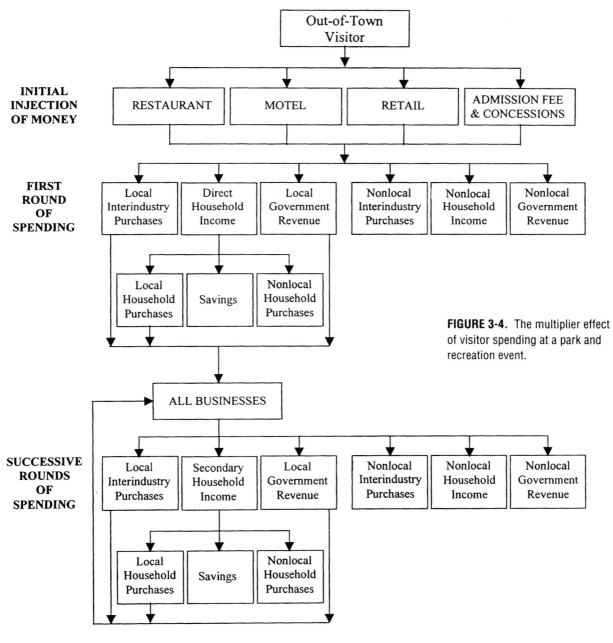

FIGURE 3-4. The multiplier effect of visitor spending at a park and recreation event.

The multiplier process is shown in Figure 3-4. To illustrate the process, the figure assumes that visitors spend their money at four different types of establishments in a community. Their initial injection of money constitutes the *direct* economic impact on the community. Figure 3-4 shows the six different ways in which each of the establishments receiving the initial funds could disburse the money it receives:

1) With other private sector businesses in the same jurisdiction (local interindustry purchases) to restock inventories to provide for future sales; to maintain buildings, fittings and equipment; to pay insurance premiums; and for a myriad of other purposes

2) With employees or shareholders who reside within the community in the form of salaries and wages or dividends constituting personal income for them (direct household income)

3) With local governments as sales taxes, property taxes, and license fees (local government revenue)

4) With private sector businesses located outside the local jurisdiction (nonlocal, interindustry purchases)

5) With employees or shareholders who reside outside the community in the form of salaries and wages or dividends constituting personal income for them (nonlocal household income)

6) With nonlocal (e.g., state and federal) governments as sales taxes or taxes on profits

Three different types of economic impact measures are commonly reported, and all of them use multiplier coefficients. They are sales, personal income, and employment.

The latter three categories of spending illustrate that the host city is part of a larger economy, and some money leaks out of the community's economic system to pay taxes to, or buy goods and services from, entities outside the community. Only those dollars remaining within the host community after leakage has taken place constitute the net economic gain to it. The amount of the initial expenditures that remains in the jurisdiction from local interindustry purchases, direct household income, and local government revenue is subsequently spent in one of the six ways previously listed and thereby sets in motion a further chain of economic activity.

Interpreting alternative measures of economic impact. Three different types of economic impact measures are commonly reported, and all of them use multiplier coefficients. They are sales, personal income, and employment. Because the first two of these are measured in dollars, they are often confused. A sales or output measure reports the effects of an extra unit of visitor spending on economic activity within a host community. It relates visitor expenditure to the increase in business turnover that it creates. This rather esoteric measure has very limited practical value. It may be of some interest to economists interested in researching industry interdependencies, to business proprietors interested in sales impacts, or to officials in governmental entities interested in approximating sales revenues that may accrue from injections of funds into particular sectors, but it does not offer insights useful for guiding policy decisions of local elected officials.

The *personal income* measure of economic impact reports the effect of an extra unit of visitor spending on the level of personal income in the host community. In contrast to the sales output indicator, the income measure has substantial practical implications for stakeholders because it enables them to relate the economic benefits received by residents to the money they invested (see Figure 3-3 on page 35 for a graphic description of this relationship).

In an analysis of the impact of a park and recreation facility or event, sales measures of economic impact are unlikely to be of interest to local residents. The point of interest is likely to be the impact of visitors' expenditures on residents' personal incomes. Most government officials and taxpayers are likely to be interested only in knowing how much extra income residents will receive from the injection of funds from visitors. Their interest in value of sales per se is likely to be limited because it does not directly affect residents' standard of living. Furthermore, the use of sales indicators may give a false impression of the true impacts of visitor spending because the highest effects on personal income are not necessarily generated from the highest increases in sales.

The conceptual model shown in Figure 3-3, which illustrates the rationale for economic impact studies, specifies that their purpose is to compare the amount of money residents invest in a park and recreation event or facility with the amount of income they receive from it. The notion of sales transactions does not appear anywhere in the model, and from the perspective of residents and elected officials, it is irrelevant to the analysis. Nevertheless, because sales measures of economic impact are frequently three or more times larger than personal income indicators, sponsors of economic impact studies invariably report economic impact in terms of sales outputs rather than personal income. The higher numbers appear to justify better the public investment that is being advocated, but they are meaningless for this purpose.

Careful Interpretation of Employment Measures

An *employment* multiplier coefficient measures the effect of an extra unit of visitor spending on employment in the host community. Three important caveats regarding the estimates of employment should be noted.

First, estimates usually include both full-time and part-time jobs and frequently do not distinguish between them. The employment measure commonly does not identify the number of hours worked in each job or the proportion of jobs that are full and part time. Thus, decision makers easily may be misled into assuming that all jobs are full-time positions.

Second, the employment estimates assume that all existing employees are fully occupied, so an increase in external visitor spending will require an increase in level of employment within the jurisdiction. In the context of the front desk of a hotel, for example, the employment estimator assumes that the existing staff would be unable to handle additional guests checking in for overnight stays associated with a recreation event. In many cases, however, those desk staff are sufficiently underemployed to handle additional workload, so additional staff would not be needed. In these situations, the employment coefficient is exaggerated.

A third potentially misleading corollary of employment estimates is that they imply that community residents will fill all the new jobs created. It is possible, however, that nonresidents will fill a proportion of these new jobs.

A REVIEW OF THE ECONOMIC IMPACT OF 19 RECREATION EVENTS

The author of this report was responsible for identifying the economic impact of 19 recreation events held during a 2-year period in 8 cities. The eight cities are profiled in Figure 3-5. The data were collected using the questionnaire shown in Figure 3-6, and the multipliers were calculated using the IMPLAN input-output modeling system. This software system is relatively inexpensive (usually less than $1,000), relatively easy to use, and is readily available and accessible.

Name	Location	Population Size	Income ($) Median
Boise	State capital and one of two metropolitan areas in Idaho	168,000	36,000
College Station	Brazos County, Texas, equidistant between Houston and Austin	66,000	29,000
Des Moines	The political, economic, and cultural capital of Iowa, located in the heart of the state	200,000	42,000
Everett	The largest city in SnohomishCounty, Washington	80,000	46,000
Grand Rapids	West Michigan	192,000	44,000
Lansing	South-central lower Michigan, 90 miles west of Detroit	125,000	27,000
Ocean City	Seaside resort town on the Atlantic coast, Maryland	7,388	40,600*
Scottsdale	In the Sonoran Desert at the base of the McDougall Mountains, Arizona	200,000	50,000

* Worcester County median income

FIGURE 3-5. Profile of the study cities.

A summary of results from the 19 recreation events that were studied is given in Figure 3-7. To avoid the possibility of embarrassment to any of the cooperating cities, their identities have been protected and have been replaced by the letter symbols shown in the left-hand column. Columns 2 and 3 list the names of the events and their duration in days, respectively.

Economic impact refers only to the expenditures of visitors from outside the community who were attracted there by the event. In other words, the expenditures of those residing inside the city (columns 6 and 7) as well as casuals and time switchers (columns 8 and 9) have been excluded.

The total expenditures shown in column 12 are derived from two sources: (1) the number of visitors who were attracted to the community by the event; and (2) the incremental amount spent by casuals and time-switchers that could be attributed to an extension of their stay in the community because of the event. Columns 14, 15, and 16 report the three economic impact measures discussed in the previous section: sales, personal income, and jobs.

The data in Figure 3-7 suggest the following:

• Large numbers of participants and spectators do not necessarily equate to a large economic impact. For example, the Street Rod Run in city A and the Golf Tournament in city D, shown near the bottom of the list in Figure 3-7, attracted only 1,409 and 1,259 visitors, respectively. In contrast, the 4th of July Celebration in city F and Minor League Baseball games in city C attracted 55,000 and 16,895 visitors, respectively. The economic impacts of the Street Rod Run and Golf Tournament events, however, were substantially greater than those accruing from the 4th of July Celebration or Minor League Base-

FIGURE 3-6. Economic impact questionnaire.

1. What is the zip code at your home address? _____

2. Which of the following days will you be at this event? (Please circle *all* that apply)
    <u>Friday</u>   <u>Saturday</u>   <u>Sunday</u>

3. How many people (**including yourself**) are in your immediate group? (This is the number of people for whom you typically pay the bills; for example, your family or close friends) _____ people

---

Alternative questions 1 and 2 to be used (question 3 is omitted) in the context of a sports tournament
1. What is the name of your team? _____

2. How many players are there on your team at this tournament? _____

---

4. To better understand the economic impact of the [Name of Event], we are interested in finding out the approximate amount of money you and other visitors in your immediate group will spend, including travel to and from your home. We understand that this is a difficult question, but please do your best because your responses are very important to our efforts. **DURING THE COURSE OF YOUR VISIT, WHAT IS THE APPROXIMATE AMOUNT <u>YOUR IMMEDIATE GROUP</u> WILL SPEND IN EACH OF THE FOLLOWING CATEGORIES:**

TYPE OF EXPENDITURE	Amount spent in the [name of city] area	Amount spent outside the [name of city] area
A. Admission / Entry Fees	_____	_____
B. Food & Beverages (restaurants, concessions, etc.)	_____	_____
C. Lounges & Bars (cover charges, drinks, etc.)	_____	_____
D. Retail Shopping (clothing, souvenirs, gifts, etc.)	_____	_____
E. Lodging Expenses (hotel, motel, etc.)	_____	_____
F. Private Auto Expenses (gas, oil, repairs, parking fees, etc.)	_____	_____
G Rental Car Expenses	_____	_____
H. Any Other Expenses	_____	_____

Please identify: _____

Questions 5 and 6 are not required for sports tournaments.

5. Would you have come to the [name of city] area <u>at this time</u> even if this event had not been held?
    Yes_____   No_____

    5a. If "Yes", did you stay longer in the [name of city] area than you would have done if this event had not been held?
    Yes_____   No_____

    5b. If "Yes" (<u>in 5a</u>), how much longer? _____Days

6. Would you have come to [name of city] in the next three months if you had not come at this time for this event?
    Yes_____   No_____

1 City	2 Event Name	3 Duration (# of Days)	4 Mean Length of Stay of Out-of-town Visitors	5 # of Visitor Days	6 Participants/Spectators from inside the city #	7 %	8 Casuals/Time Switchers #	9 %
G	Open Golf Tournament	3	2.4	464,000	140,167	30.2	72,500	15
G	Arts Festival	1	1.8	5,000	1,765	35.3	1,588	31
G	Culinary Festival	2	1.8	35,000	9,638	27.5	11,486	32
F	Annual Arts Festival	3	1.3	500,000	414,000	82.8	40,952	8
E	Rusty Relics Car Show	1	1.2	745[a]	46	6.2	0	0
C	Two Minor League Baseball Games	1 day each	1.0	16,895	6,735	39.9	5,438	32
C	Walk at the Zoo	1	1.1	525	153	29.2	195	37
C	Yes Festival	2	3.9	6,092	3,442	56.5	560	9
D	River Festival	4	3.1	1,000,000	135,135	13.5	369,574	37
F	4th of July Gala Celebration	1	1.7	55,000	48,605	88.4	2,398	4
E	Triathlon Dash	1	1.1	482[a]	94	19.5	38	7
F	Grand Prix Motor Race	3	1.6	85,000	72,425	85.2	4,899	5
E	Nubian Jam Heritage Celebration	1	1.7	5,000	2,041	40.8	877	17
D	Women's Fitness Challenge	1	1.3	105,415[a]	83,795	79.5	0	0
A	Bluebonnet Street Rod Run	3	2.2	1,409[a]	96	6.8	0	0
D	American Junior Golf Association Tournament	4	5.4	1,259[a]	0	0.0	0	0
H	Springfest	4	2.9	101,807	22,936	22.5	35,778	35
H	Sunfest	4	3.4	179,248	26,062	14.5	66,381	37
H	Winterfest	48	1.7	58,470	18,010	30.8	15,706	26

FIGURE 3-7. The economic impact of 19 festival and spectator events.

a. The attendance data provided by the agencies for these events were in number of participants. For purposes of consistency, these were transformed in the table to number of visitor days, which includes members of participants' immediate groups.

b. This figure consists of the number of out-of-town visitors whose primary purpose of visit was to attend the event (Out-of-Towners), and the number of out-of-town visitors whose primary reason for their visit was not to attend the event but extended their stay because of it (Extended Stayers).

ball games (Columns 12 and 15). This is explained by the length of the larger events, which lasted only one day, and by the fact that only 7 percent and 28 percent of those who attended the 4th of July Celebration and baseball games, respectively, visited the communities specifically to participate in those events. Furthermore, it seems likely that many out-of-town visitors commuted to these events from nearby communities, so their spending on accommodation and food in the host communities was likely to be small.

- The importance of ascertaining the proportion of visitors who are time-switchers and casuals is clearly demonstrated in columns 8 and 9. In 7 of the 19 studies, time-switchers and casuals represented approximately one-third of all visitors. If the questionnaire had asked only for their home address or ZIP code and, therefore, failed to differentiate them from out-of-town visitors who were attracted specifically by the event, there would have been a substantial overestimation of the economic impact attributed to these events.

10	11	12	13	14	15	16
Participants/[b] spectators from outside the city		Total[c] Expenditure	Average per Visitor per Day Expenditure	Economic Impact		
#	%			Sales	Personal Income	Jobs[d]
,333	54.2	29,523,070	117	65,856,795	22,389,187	1,232.0
,647	32.9	156,664	95	336,976	113,172	6.1
3,876	39.7	540,658	39	1,175,350	397,707	21.6
5,048	9.0	462,428	10	1,037,867	357,237	22.5
699	93.8	6,562	9	12,500	3,894	0.3
,722	27.9	25,225	5	54,184	17,818	1.3
177	33.7	548	3	1,055	345	0.0
2,090	34.3	56,650	27	111,616	36,643	2.6
5,291	49.5	5,781,136	12	14,698,137	4,442,505	326.0
3,997	7.3	34,420	9	74,793	25,474	1.5
350	72.6	14,841	42	25,693	11,416	0.5
7,676	9.0	172,764	23	382,446	129,902	7.8
2,082	41.7	32,356	16	64,715	19,678	1.4
,620	20.5	559,246	26	892,808	429,238	23.9
,313	93.2	55,233	42	104,333	31,980	2.4
,259	100.0	74,868	59	188,414	56,690	4.0
,093	42.3	1,922,382	45	2,655,348	1,100,942	61.2
,805	48.5	3,873,727	45	5,360,853	2,200,907	121.0
,754	42.4	883,557	36	1,217,565	503,876	28.4

c. This figure consists of the expenditures by out-of-town visitors and extended stayers.

d. This figure refers to both full-time and part-time jobs. It assumes the local economy is operating at full capacity and that there is no slack to absorb additional demand created by these events.

- Reasonably accurate measures of economic impact depend on reasonably accurate counts of visitors to the events because the impact estimates are derived by extrapolating from a sample to a total visitation count. In sports tournaments where teams or individuals have to register with the organizers, an accurate count is usually available. Similarly, at gated spectator or festival events that charge an admission, accurate counts are available from ticket sales and/or turnstile counts. However, many festivals are not gated and do not charge admission. In these cases, attendance counts are frequently guesstimates made by the organizers. If these are inaccurate, the economic impacts will be inaccurate. For example, if the River Festival attendance in Figure 3-7 were actually 200,000 rather than 1 million, the total expenditure would be $1.15 million rather than $5.78 million! (Note: In fact, there was no reason to question the accuracy of this estimate of 1 million in attendance in this case. That discrepancy was selected to illustrate the point.) Accuracy in sampling, data collection, and analysis is of little use if the total attendance counts are inaccurate.

Event Name	Date	Duration (# of Days)	# of Visitor Days	Participants/ Spectators from inside the city		Casuals/Time Switchers	
				#	%	#	%
Annual Arts Festival	6-5	3	500,000	414,000	82.8	40,952	8.
4th of July Gala Celebration	7-4	1	55,000	48,605	88.4	2,398	4.
Grand Prix Motor Race	7-24	3	85,000	72,425	85.2	4,899	5.
WinterFest	1-23	2	16,000	13,674	85.5	976	6.
Three Fires Pow Wow	6-13	2	25,000	21,365	85.5	1,525	6.
African-American Festival	7-10	3	15,000	12,819	85.5	915	6.
Jazz & Blues Festival	7-31	2	10,000	8,546	85.5	610	6.
Italian Festival	8-7	3	30,000	25,638	85.5	1,830	6.
Polish Harvest Festival	8-28	3	15,000	12,819	85.5	915	6.
German Festival	9-4	3	10,000	8,546	85.5	610	6.
Celebration on the Grand	9-11	2	350,000	299,110	85.5	21,350	6.
Hispanic Festival	9-11	3	70,000	59,822	85.5	4,270	6.
Mexican Festival	9-18	3	100,000	85,460	85.5	6,100	6.
Total	-	-	1,281,000	1,082,829		87,350	

FIGURE 3-8. The economic impact of special events held in City F.

a. This figure consists of the number of out-of-town visitors whose primary purpose of visit was to attend the event (out-of-towners), and the number of out-of-town visitors whose primary reason for their visit was not to attend the event but extended their stay because of it (Extended Stayers).

b. This figure consists of the expenditures by out-of-town visitors and extended stayers.

- The extraordinary economic impact generated in a local community by a mega-event (as opposed to a typical community festival) is demonstrated by the first event listed in Figure 3-7. This golf tournament was a stop on the men's professional tour. The very high total expenditure (column 12) not only reflects the number of people staying multiple nights in the community and a large proportion of visitors from out of town, but also shows that the visitors were relatively affluent. The near $30 million estimate in Figure 3-7 is limited to the expenditures of spectators and does not include those by: the players, officials, and their entourages; the extensive number of media representatives; the hospitality expenditures of major companies; and sponsorships. Nevertheless, the $30 million expenditure dwarfs the aggregated $14.6 million generated by the other 18 festivals and events shown in Figure 3-7.

- If an overnight stay is not required, the economic impact on the community is likely to be relatively small. The per capita expenditures at one-day events by out-of-town visitors were $95, $9, $5, $3, $9, $42, $16, and $26 (column 13). The three largest numbers had features that made them atypical one-day events. At the Arts Festival, emphasis was on selling art rather than only viewing it. The $95 amount reflects this retailing dimension. Both the Triathlon Dash ($42) and the Women's Fitness Challenge ($26) had an overnight component, even though they were one-day events. Many participants arrived in the community the previous evening so they would be rested before participating in the next day's athletic event.

Participants/[a] Spectators from outside the city		Total[b] Expenditure	Economic Impact		
#	%		Sales	Personal Income	Jobs[c]
45,048	9.0	462,428	1,037,867	357,237	22.5
3,997	7.3	34,420	74,793	25,474	1.5
7,676	9.0	172,764	382,446	129,902	7.8
1,350	8.4	18,623	28,724	11,025	0.6
2,110	8.4	29,107	44,894	17,231	0.9
1,266	8.4	17,464	26,936	10,339	0.5
844	8.4	11,643	17,958	6,893	0.4
2,532	8.4	34,929	53,874	20,678	1.1
1,266	8.4	17,464	26,936	10,339	0.5
844	8.4	11,643	17,958	6,893	0.4
29,540	8.4	407,504	628,529	241,239	12.7
5,908	8.4	81,501	125,706	48,248	2.5
8,440	8.4	116,430	179,580	68,926	3.6
110,821		1,415,920	2,646,201	954,424	55.0

c. This figure refers to both full-time and part-time jobs. It assumes the local economy is operating at full capacity and that there is no slack to absorb additional demand created by these events.

PRESENTING ECONOMIC IMPACT RESULTS TO MAKE THE ECONOMIC CASE

Those agencies and organizations responsible for parks and recreation should prepare an annual economic impact report for their stakeholders, a report similar to ones prepared by many tourism agencies. Extrapolations can be made from events in the community that were surveyed to other events that were not.

An annual balance sheet showing the economic impact of recreation events sponsored by city F is shown in Figure 3-8. It was derived by extrapolating results from 3 surveyed events in this city (the events listed at the top of the table) to an additional 10 city-sponsored events during the same year at which no data were collected. The percentages of visitors from inside the city, casuals/time switchers, and visitors from outside the city were similar at all of the three surveyed events. This suggested that it was reasonable to extrapolate to the other events the average ratios of the 3 surveyed events of 85.5, 6.1, and 8.4 for the local residents, casuals/time switchers, and out-of-town visitors, respectively.

Attendance estimates for the 10 nonsurveyed events were available. The per capita spending by out-of-town visitors at the 3 surveyed events was $10.26 (462,428 ÷ 45,048); $8.61; and $22.50. This yielded an average of $13.79. This average was used to calculate the total expenditure at the nonsurveyed events. For example, the $18,623 total expenditure at Winter Fest was derived by using the average amount spent by each visitor times the number of out-of-town visitors ($13.79 x 1,350).

Arraying the economic return from special events in this way also offers managers and stakeholders guidelines as to which should receive priority in promotional effort. The spending of visitors to the Grand Prix was $22.50 per visitor, compared to $10.25 and $8.61 for the Arts Festival and Gala Celebration, respectively. This suggests that the most efficient strategy for city F to increase its return on investment may be to focus on out-of-town visitors to the Grand Prix rather than on the other two events.

There are many legitimate reasons for sponsoring festivals and special events beyond their contribution to economic development. However, if economic development is the prime consideration, these analyses offer a basis for prioritizing which events are most viable.

CHAPTER 4

Attracting Businesses

Increased business activity typically means more jobs, a higher level of housing starts, and more revenue for states and communities, which in turn contributes to better schools, parks, cultural institutions, and health services.

There is a widespread perception that the well-being of communities is substantially dependent upon ecnomic growth. With relatively few exceptions, such as the location of military, academic, religious, or political establishments, this economic growth is fostered by the location of businesses. Company start-ups, expansions, and relocations are widely viewed as direct and effective means of enhancing a community's economic development through expanding its existing tax base. Many believe the multiplier effect ensures that the benefits from a new business spread throughout a community and extend far beyond the actual dollar value of a firm's initial investment and subsequent payroll. Increased business activity typically means more jobs, a higher level of housing starts, and more revenue for states and communities, which in turn contributes to better schools, parks, cultural institutions, and health services.

Substantial shifts in American industry have occurred in recent decades with the change from traditional manufacturing to "smokeless" industries. Related to this has been a shift in emphasis from attracting new companies toward accommodating the relocation and expansion needs of existing companies. This shift reflects "the mounting evidence that the vast majority of new jobs generated in the United States came from existing companies and new business start-ups" (Kotler, Haider, and Rein 1993, 247).

Many of the smokeless industries may be characterized as "footloose" because they are likely to be less constrained and more flexible in their choice of location than traditional manufacturing companies. They are not tied to raw materials, natural resources, or energy supplies, meaning that cities seeking ways to expand their tax base see them as excellent prospects for relocation. They are companies whose financial performance is relatively independent of location decisions and whose principal resource typically is their employees. Footloose companies are particularly attractive to communities because they infuse money into a local economy without adverse effects (e.g., pollution) often associated with traditional manufacturing industries. Further, footloose businesses tend to offer higher levels of compensation than blue-collar companies. The perceived importance of footloose companies to tax base growth is emphasized by the aggressiveness with which jurisdictions actively recruit and compete for these entities. Their emerging dominance has created a highly competitive environment among communities seeking to expand their tax base (Festervand et al. 1988). One of the most profound changes to occur in the industrial environment in the last decade has been the unbridled pursuit of new industries by public and private economic development organizations. These organizations are estimated to exceed 10,000 in number with recruitment budgets in excess of $300 million.

The representatives of the footloose company ranked quality of life as the most important of the location elements listed, whereas the manufacturing and distribution company officials ranked it ninth out of 11 elements.

Megan Lewis

THE ROLE OF QUALITY OF LIFE

Researchers have shown that the elements that are important in location decisions for footloose companies are different from those considered to be important by those in manufacturing and distribution firms. For example, Rex (1990) compared how officials in research and development, high technology, and headquarters operations ranked 11 elements related to location decisions to the rankings of those elements by decision makers in manufacturing and distribution facilities. The representatives of the footloose company ranked quality of life as the most important of the location elements listed, whereas the manufacturing and distribution company officials ranked it ninth out of 11 elements.

The economic success of many businesses depends on their work force. This is particularly true of those businesses in the intensely recruited high technology, research and development, and company headquarters categories. Their principal assets are ideas and a skilled workforce, rather than their inventories and capital equipment. These types of "people-intensive" businesses (Festervand et al. 1988) are information factories whose viability relies on their ability to attract and retain highly educated professional employees. The deciding factor for such individuals in choosing where to work is often the quality of life in the geographic vicinity of the business. A vice-president of Dell Corporation in Austin, Texas, one of the country's largest computer suppliers, observed:

> People working in high-tech companies are used to there being a high quality of life in the metropolitan areas in which they live. When we at Dell go and recruit in those areas, we have to be able to demonstrate to them that the quality of life in Austin is at least comparable or they won't come. It's about what's the community like where I'm going to live (Crompton 1999b, 8).

Scanlon (1984) notes that these businesses understand that if a business selects a site that meets the sociopsychological needs of the workforce, its employees will be better prepared to meet the company's operating needs. Taylor (1987) supported this line of reasoning. He asserted that the quality of employees' lives has a direct impact on an employer's bottom line through absenteeism, loyalty, turnover, productivity, and health-care costs.

In a bygone era, businesses often gravitated to places that had low taxes and few services (Kotler et al. 1993). Now, however, many types of industries secure these advantages by locating in underdeveloped countries. Hence, footloose companies in the United States are often drawn to places that offer high-quality services. Operating costs are rarely a consideration, for example, in high-tech industry location decisions (Kotler et al.1993). Quality of life and community attractiveness to engineers and scientists have emerged as major variables in siting firms. Businesses tend to have a nucleus of key personnel who are critical to their successful operation, and their ability to attract or retain these key individuals is important in defining that company's economic future (Glaser and Bardo 1991).

While financial packages from communities may be a necessary qualifying element in attracting companies, they are usually not the differentiating or determining element because the financial packages from competing communities are likely to be similar (Decker and Crompton 1993).

No matter how quality of life is defined, park and recreational opportunities are likely to be a major component of it. There are no great cities in North America or elsewhere in the world that do not have great park, recreation, and cultural amenities.

The importance of quality of life in business location decisions has been repeatedly verified in the literature (Boyle 1988; Bramlage 1988; Carn and Rabianski 1991; Conway 1985; Epping 1986; Sarvis 1989; Tosh et al.1988). It is widely cited as being especially important for high-technology firms or businesses employing highly skilled workers in information- or knowledge-based services (Myers 1987). Blair and Premus (1987) conclude from their review of the company relocation literature that the continued shift to more advanced technologies will lead to an increase in the importance of quality-of-life factors and a relative decrease in the significance of more traditional determinants.

There is a substantial economic literature on the need for "disamenity compensation," whereby companies in jurisdictions with a less favorable quality of life have to pay higher salaries in order to attract the same quality worker, and vice-versa (Myers 1987; Power 1980). The overall implication is that firms can reduce the salary levels needed to secure adequate labor (or secure more and better workers at the same price) if they locate in an area whose quality of life is attractive to workers (Myers 1987). Quality of life is not only important in relocation, expansion, or initiation decisions, it is also important in employee retention and has an economic bottom line—it is expensive to go through the recruitment process, particularly for key personnel.

Clearly, the elements that differentiate one jurisdiction from another are increasingly related to what a community can offer in quality of life. If a community commits to a long-term comprehensive plan to enhance the factors that it can control and that positively influence quality of life, it is likely to have an advantage over other places when recruiting and retaining business.

THE ROLE OF RECREATION AND PARKS IN QUALITY OF LIFE

No matter how quality of life is defined, park and recreational opportunities are likely to be a major component of it. There are no great cities in North America or elsewhere in the world that do not have great park, recreation, and cultural amenities. Great is defined not in terms of size but in terms of people's desire to live there. Great park, recreation, and cultural amenities are synonymous with great cities.

Glaser and Bardo (1991), in a study of 700 chief executive officers, examined 10 quality-of-life attributes for their relative importance in the attraction or retention of key personnel. They found that well-developed community spirit and entertainment opportunities were the "greatest lures" for businesses. Similarly, Festervand et al. (1988) reported that members of the American Economic Development Council perceived recreational opportu-

Scanlon discussed open spaces and contact with the natural world in terms of "sensory quality" . . . as essential in the total process: "A community that would attract a growth industry will preserve its visual distinctiveness and open space."

Megan Lewis

nities to be relatively important to locating companies, along with cultural and social opportunities. In a study of 226 high-technology firms located in southern California, Galbraith and DeNoble (1988) compared location decisions made by companies of differing size, industry type, and institutional form. Culture, climate, density, recreational activities, and schools proved to be the most important "ambiance" elements among high-technology companies. Furthermore, smaller companies reported they were more concerned with ambiance factors than were larger firms. The study by Snepenger et al. (1995, 42) of 420 business owners and managers in Montana reported that they "did not consider business climate values to be as important as community setting, natural environment, and recreational opportunity values."

Scanlon (1984) discussed open spaces and contact with the natural world in terms of "sensory quality." He identified sensory quality as essential in the total process: "A community that would attract a growth industry will preserve its visual distinctiveness and open space" (p. 21). The vice-president of a large high-tech corporation in Austin, Texas, reiterated this point in Crompton (1999b, 9):

> We have a labor shortage in Austin. From an industry point of view, it is imperative that we create a living environment that all kinds of people find attractive. That is, generation X'ers, Y'ers, families and so on. They all want recreation opportunities. People talk about the recreation amenities of Town Lake and that was fine for a city of 250,000, but Austin is soon going to have a million people. Development is going where everyone wants to go to recreate: streams, rivers, hills and so on. This creates a problem for us in recruiting people. They want to hike, bike, boat, picnic, and so on, and the opportunities aren't there. Many of the opportunities on lakes and waterways are being closed off by private development and access is increasingly difficult.

Crompton, Love, and More (1997) studied the importance of park, recreation, and open space amenities to key decision makers from 174 businesses that had relocated, expanded, or been launched in Colorado in a five-year period. In developing their sample, the researchers were cognizant of the need to avoid Harding's (1989) two principal criticisms of previous studies of business location decisions.

First, Harding noted that the studies had gathered their information from individuals who were not considering a location decision at that time: "It reflects what a decision maker believes would be important if he were to make a decision" (p. 223). He argued that such responses are likely to be superficial because respondents have had no reason to give the issue thoughtful consideration. Therefore, Crompton, Love, and Moore chose a sample restricted to decision makers in businesses that had initiated, expanded, or relocated operations to Colorado in the five-year period prior to the study. These respondents would almost certainly have had to give serious thought to the relative importance of location elements to their companies. At the request of the researchers, officials from the state's 87 economic development agencies and chambers of commerce identified companies that met this criterion.

Harding's second criticism was that the individual in a company who was the real decision maker on location issues was often not the same individual who completed the survey. To minimize the possibility of this happening, the researchers in the Crompton, Love, and Moore study contacted each business in the sample by telephone. The telephone conversation determined each company's eligibility for inclusion in the study, identified the name of the key person who had been most involved in the relocation decision-making process, solicited his or her cooperation for the study, and verified the mailing address.

Respondents were asked to allocate 100 points among the six elements on each of the two constant sum scales that were designed to identify the relative importance of general elements and the relative importance of quality-of-life elements in influencing location decisions. Particular emphasis in the study was given to investigating differences in criteria based on the size of businesses because previous studies had suggested that this was likely to be substantial.

For example, Galbraith and DeNoble (1988) reported differences in the importance of location factors between small and large companies. Haug and Ness (1993) reported that more than 91 percent of the biotechnology firms in their sample cited founder preference as either very important or important in the location choice. It seems likely that the founder's influence will be substantially more pronounced in smaller companies than in larger companies because the latter are likely to be longer established and have a relatively large number of shareholders who dilute the founder's influence even if he or she is still an owner.

Elements	Small Company Mean (n=38)	Large Company Mean (n=42)
Government Incentives	3.9	14.2
Quality of Life	33.3	14.7
Labor	10.3	24/0
Proximity to Customers	28.4	11.6
Operating Costs	17.2	24.3
Transportation	6.7	7.7

TABLE 4-1. Comparison of perceptions of the relative importance of general elements in location decisions between decisions makers in large and small companies.

Researchers compared the answers from companies in the smallest quartile of the sample (defined by the number of full-time personnel; "small" meant companies with fewer than 8 employees) with responses from companies in the highest quartile (employing 88 or more people full-time). Emphatic differences emerged between the two groups in their ratings of the general location elements (Table 4-1). Large companies were significantly more concerned with "government incentives" and "labor" issues than were small companies, while small companies assigned substantially more importance to "quality of life" and "proximity to customers" than did larger companies.

Elements	Small Company Mean (n=38)	Large Company Mean (n=42)
Primary/Secondary Education	19.4	18.0
Recreation/Parks/Open Spaces	26.4	12.1
Cost of Living/Housing	23.0	34.5
Personal Safety/Crime Rate	12.9	13.2
Cultural Opportunities	10.6	9.5
Health/Medical Services	7.1	9.2

TABLE 4-2. Comparison of perceptions of the relative importance of quality-of-life elements in location decisions in large and small companies.

When researchers analyzed the relative importance of quality-of-life elements, they also found substantial and significant differences between the two groups on the emphasis given to "recreation/parks/open spaces" and to the "cost of living/housing" (Table 4-2). While the predominant concern of large companies was with the bottom-line costs of locating in an area, decision makers in small companies ranked "recreation/parks/

open space" as their highest priority. The preference for a good quality of life and recreation/parks/open spaces among decision makers in small companies may be explained in economic terms by the concept of "satisficing" (a balance between satisfaction and sacrifice) introduced more than 40 years ago by Herbert Simon (1957). Simon asserted that some companies set profit goals for themselves that are not the optimum but are merely "good enough." Sometimes a company could earn higher profits than it does, but this would involve adverse trade-offs for its employees and owners in their quality of life. Thus, Simon argued, they satisfice; that is, they accept a somewhat lower level of profits.

The preference for a good quality of life and recreation/ parks/open spaces among decision makers in small companies may be explained in economic terms by the concept of "satisficing" (a balance between satisfaction and sacrifice).

This type of trade-off may be more difficult for larger companies, especially if they are accountable to a number of investors or stockholders who are not directly involved in management of the company and whose only concern is maximizing investment. Many small company owners, who are responsible only to themselves may settle for a level of profits that is "good enough" and permits them to enjoy a preferred life style. One observer commented, "The new breed of entrepreneur is less like the swashbuckler out for the quick hit and more like the pilgrim looking for a better life" (Selz 1994, B2).

These findings appear to reaffirm the central contribution of recreation activities to life satisfaction that has long been articulated (Iso-Ahola 1980). The priority given to recreation/parks/open spaces by small businesses is particularly significant given the trends in job creation. Although not all agree (Harrison 1994), there appears to be widespread acceptance that, throughout the United States in recent times, employment growth in small businesses has outpaced job growth in large businesses. Approximately 90 percent of all businesses employ fewer than 10 people (U.S. Department of Commerce 1992).

THE RELATIONSHIP BETWEEN PARKS ADVOCATES AND ECONOMIC DEVELOPMENT AGENCIES

As is clear from the empirical evidence offered above, park and recreational opportunities play a role in the location decisions of many of the businesses communities vigorously recruit. Typically, however, the agencies and organizations responsible for parks acquisition, siting, maintenance, and programming are not invited to be directly involved in economic development work in their cities. At least part of the reason for this may be an underestimation by economic development personnel of the importance of recreation/parks/open spaces in location decisions.

Decker and Crompton (1990; 1993) recognize that there may be a discrepancy between the factors that economic development officials believe are important to companies in location decisions and what decision makers in the companies actually consider to be important. They suggest that this might reflect the "outsider" role of economic development organizations, which are not likely to be intimately involved in the location evaluation process:

> The major limitation associated with economic development professionals is that they are involved in the decision process only peripherally, serving as conduits through which to provide information when invited to do so. Hence, they are not in a strategic position to fully understand the process or the key attributes in a location decision. (Decker and Crompton 1990, 39)

In the Colorado business relocation study described above, researchers also solicited the views of key individuals at 73 economic development agencies on the relative importance of the general and quality-of-life elements that defined the study. Comparisons of their views and those of the company relocation personnel are shown in Tables 4-3 and 4-4.

General Elements	Agency Respondent Mean (n=73)	Company Respondent Mean (n=174)
Government Incentives	12.6	9.3
Quality of Life	18.9	21.9
Labor	19.2	17.6
Proximity to Customers	11.4	20.6
Operating Costs	23.7	20.7
Transportation	14.2	9.3

TABLE 4-3. Perceived importance of general elements in location decisions by economic development and company respondents.

Quality-of-Life Elements	Small Company Mean (n=73)	Large Company Mean (n=174)
Primary/Secondary Education	25.8	16.6
Recreation/Parks/Open Spaces	13.1	18.1
Cost of Living/Housing	25.6	28.8
Personal Safety/Crime Rate	12.7	16.3
Cultural Opportunities	8.3	9.9
Health/Medical Services	14.5	10.3

TABLE 4-4. Perceived importance of quality-of-life elements in location decisions by economic development agency and business respondents.

Of the six general location elements, company respondents rated "quality of life" highest, but it was closely followed by "operating costs," "proximity to customers," and "labor." Economic development agency respondents rated "quality of life" third, but the magnitude of the difference in mean scores between the two groups on this element was not significant. The only significant differences between the two groups were the weight given to "proximity to customers" and to "transportation." However, on the quality-of-life scale (Table 4-4), economic development agencies significantly underestimated the relative importance that businesses placed on "recreation/parks/open space," "personal safety/crime rate," and "cultural opportunities."

In addition to economic development officials often not being deeply involved in a company's relocation decision-making process, this discrepancy in the appreciation of the importance of the role of parks and recreation may be attributable to economic development officials being primarily focused on recruiting large companies. If that's the case, they may not be as sensitive to the different priorities of small businesses when it comes to making decisions about location. Whatever the reason for their lack of awareness of the priority placed on recreation/parks/open space, it appears to exist. Hence, it is incumbent upon those responsible for parks and recreation to communicate the important role of these amenities to elected officials and economic development organizations by using testimonials from companies in their own community.

CONCLUDING COMMENTS

The profound influence that park and recreation amenities have on people's preferred living locations can be illustrated by a simple exercise that the author has undertaken with literally hundreds of different groups. First, all members of the group are asked to write the place that they would like to live given their druthers (that is, their preferred place, ignoring pragmatic concerns, such as job, family, language, and heritage). After this task has been completed, each of them is asked to write in one sentence why they picked that place. When responses to this second task are analyzed, results are invariably similar. More than 80 percent of participants will cite some dimension of park, recreational, or environmental ambiance in their responses.

For many people, once they attain a threshold level of income, improvements in quality of lifestyle become more important than increases in salary. The amenities of a location constitute "the second paycheck." For example, a $15,000 raise in salary may not be sufficient to persuade a professional who has strong social networks in Place A, where he or she earns $70,000 with a company, to move to a similar company in Place B if the location offers similar lifestyle opportunities. However, the same individual may be enticed to move from the company in Place A to a similar job in Place C for a $5,000 salary increase if Place C offers superior lifestyle opportunities. Because park and recreation amenities are important lifestyle elements to many, it is not surprising that many company representatives recognize them as being important in attracting and retaining professional and executive employees.

Real repositioning (Chapter 1) requires that park advocates become part of a community's strategic marketing effort to attract businesses. Too few park and recreation organizations show an interest in their community's efforts to recruit and retain businesses. If they become involved in these efforts, it draws attention to the role that parks, recreation, and open space play in the relocation decisions of some companies. Their involvement should extend to identifying the facilities and services that businesses seek and to advocating that they be provided as part of the community's economic development effort. The importance of community ambiance in business location decisions provides park advocates with leverage to advocate community commitment to such features as greenways, urban tree planting, underground rather than surface wiring, tree protection ordinances, and substantial exaction requirements. This is especially true for the planning department, which is responsible for many of these urban design initiatives and standards.

Strategic place marketing involves "designing a community to satisfy the needs of its stakeholders. . . . If small business constitutes the engine of the job generation process, then places should promote those things that facilitate small business growth" (Kotler et al. 1993, 12). Historically, most jurisdictions have been product-driven rather than market-driven in their efforts to persuade companies to locate in their communities; namely, they have focused on selling their community as it is, rather than on adapting the community to meet the changing needs of relocating companies. This approach markedly contrasts with how most viable organizations now operate. In communities seeking to attract footloose companies, especially small businesses, part of a market-driven approach is likely to involve real repositioning by investing in park and recreation amenities.

Reliance on substantial tax and cash incentives to attract businesses is risky because these incentives are transient. If a community is not an engaging place in which to live, companies are likely to continue looking for the next set of cash and tax incentives, and will move on when they are offered. If a community's amenities are of a high standard, it is less susceptible to such "abandonment."

Thus, a case can be made that reliance on incentives should be replaced by an alternative strategy involving community design that satisfies the needs of its key constituents. (See the sidebar featuring a recent lead edito-

> *If a community is not an engaging place in which to live, companies are likely to continue looking for the next set of cash and tax incentives.*

FOCUS ON THE GOOD LIFE
(Lead Editorial in the Des Moines Register, October 27, 1999)

**IOWA STRATEGIC PLANNERS HAVE AN OPPORTUNITY
TO MAKE PEOPLE THE PRIORITY**

The Governor's Strategic Planning Council took to the airwaves Monday evening for a statewide town meeting to gather ideas about what Iowans want their state to be like in 2010. It was a valuable exercise that was as interesting for what participants didn't say as what they did. Generally, the comments focused on the need for better education, for keeping more young people in the state, for making Iowa more welcoming to newcomers, for a cleaner environment and more cultural and recreational opportunities. Most of the comments could be lumped under a general category of improving the quality of life in Iowa.

Notably missing from the comments—at least from those that made it onto the air—was significant mention of "improving the business climate." Perhaps that's because we've been down that road before, and it led nowhere.

For the last couple of decades, Iowa policy making has been fixated on improving the business climate. The focus was on incentives to businesses, selective tax cuts for industry, and boasting about Iowa's modest wages and mostly non-union work force. The thinking was that, if businesses could be induced to bring jobs to Iowa, everything else would fall into place.

But it didn't. In almost every measure of economic gain, Iowa is near the bottom among the 50 states. Even among our Midwestern neighbors, Iowa has been bringing up the rear in income and population growth.

Meanwhile, a stagnant Iowa could look around and take note that growth occurring elsewhere wasn't necessarily happening in the states with the most favorable business climates. It was in states that are perceived to have the highest quality of life. Jobs are flowing to regions in which people find it desirable to live.

Iowa bet on the wrong strategy, and lost.

The comments heard by the Governor's Strategic Planning Council might be an indication that Iowans sense the need to change strategies. Things such as parks, recreation, cultural attractions, scenic preservation, strengthening community, cleaner water and air, and other enhancements to the quality of life, no longer can be assigned a secondary priority in Iowa. The quality of life must be the first priority. Iowa must be an inviting state not just to business, but to people. Especially to people.

rial from *The Des Moines, Iowa, Register.*) Advocates of this approach suggest that communities succeed in becoming viable "when stakeholders such as citizens, workers, and business firms derive satisfaction from their community, and when visitors, new businesses, and investors find their expectations met" (Kotler et al.1993, 18). Thus, Blair and Premus (1987), drawing conclusions from their comprehensive review of the literature on the major factors influencing industrial location, advise that government should:

> Focus its efforts on improving the overall locational attractiveness of regions. This inward-looking strategy would place primary emphasis on developing and improving local markets in skilled labor, research, risk capital, education, recreation, and cultural amenities. It would also emphasize long-run tax policy, management-labor relations, and quality-of-life factors. Industrial development would largely be a byproduct of an improved, overall business climate and a better community in which to live.

Responsibility for business recruitment in most communities has been assigned to an economic development agency. Competitive repositioning (Chapter 1) could involve subtly challenging the myth that these organizations have created about their high level of influence on company location decisions. Frequently, they claim credit for bringing XYZ company to town. The reality is that they rarely influence the company's decision. Narrowing a list of prospective communities to between two and five candidates usually occurs before community economic development organizations are contacted or have any awareness that a particular company may be planning to relocate. Typically, they become involved only in the final stage in a company's decision process. At that stage, their role is:

- to serve as a conduit through which companies conveniently can request specific information from those communities that they are considering;

- to host and coordinate visits to the community by company officials;

- to coordinate company requests for easements and planning permissions; and

- to coordinate the negotiation of incentive packages that their community is prepared to offer (Decker and Crompton 1993).

If this more limited role becomes recognized as the real function of economic development organizations, the scope of their operations may be scaled back, and these funds could be reallocated to help provide the amenities that companies seek.

Psychological repositioning (Chapter 1) could involve soliciting testimonials from senior executives of companies that have relocated. These testimonials to the role of park and recreation amenities in relocation decisions can be persuasive. In many decision-making public forums, emotion plays an important role, and having this personal "evidence" can be important elements in repositioning a department.

CHAPTER 5

Attracting and Retaining Retirees

In terms of per-capita disposable income in the United States, the 55-to-59, 60-to-64, and 65-to-69 age cohorts are wealthier than any other 5-year age-range cohorts.

n the mid-1930s, when the Social Security system was established, life expectancy was approximately 60 years at birth and about 12 years more for those who were already 60. In other words, with the Social Security retirement age set at 65, the system typically would pay benefits for about another 7 years. By the year 2000, all of these parameters had expanded dramatically. Life expectancy in the U.S. was 76 years at birth while those aged 65 could expect to live an additional 18 years (Wiatrowski 2001). Approximately 1 in 7 Americans were 65 years or older in 2000, and this ratio is projected to increase to 1 in 4 by the year 2050 according to current U.S. Bureau of the Census projections.

To accommodate this extended period of life in later years, Social Security was supplemented with a host of private retirement benefit plans funded both by employers and by individuals. As a result, a growing proportion of retirees are relatively wealthy. Indeed, in terms of per-capita disposable income in the United States, the 55-to-59, 60-to-64, and 65-to-69 age cohorts are wealthier than any other 5-year age-range cohorts.

A third trend complementing increased longevity and enhanced income is earlier retirement. The concept of retirement is not easy to define. It could imply eligibility for benefits, withdrawal from the labor force, reduction from full-time to part-time labor, changes in life style, changes in family or living situations, or some combination of these characteristics (Wiatrowski 2001). However, a key indicator for the purposes of this chapter is the proportion of older people in the labor force. This has fallen dramatically. For example, in 1948 almost 50 percent of all men age 65 or older were in the labor force, but by 2000 this proportion had fallen below 14 percent.

Most retirees do age in place or remain in the same area where they spent much of their lives. Between 1985 and 1990, however, more than 1.9 million Americans age 60 or older changed their state of residence. The states receiving most in-migration from this group were Florida (24 percent), California (7 percent), Arizona (5 percent), and Texas (4 percent) (Longino 1995). Although the Sunbelt states of the South experienced the most substantial increase in elderly populations in the past decade, other areas also received substantial in-migration of elderly persons, including the Ozarks of Arkansas, the woods of North Wisconsin and Michigan, the mountains of Colorado and Montana, the Puget Sound Area of Washington State, and the coast of New England (U.S. Bureau of the Census 1992).

The U.S. Department of Agriculture defines nonmetropolitan retirement counties as those in which the population age 60 and over in 1990 was at least 15 percent higher than it would have been without the in-migration of older people from 1980 to 1990. Based on the 1990 census data. One-fifth of all nonmetropolitan counties are classified as retirement counties (Fagan and Longino 1993). At the time of writing, the 2000 census data were not available, but it seems likely this trend has continued in the past decade.

Communities that have invested substantial effort in trying to expand their tax base by attracting new businesses are recognizing that recruiting these mobile, retiring persons as new permanent residents may be an effective complementary strategy.

Members of this mobile retiree cohort have been termed "GRAMPIES" (Growing [number of] Retired Active Monied People In Excellent Shape) (Van der Merwe 1987). Several studies have reported that mobile retirees generally fit the GRAMPIES profile (Biggar 1980; Wiseman and Roseman 1979; Litwak and Longino 1987; Warnes 1982). Van der Merwe (1987) cites several trends, validated by Census reports, that have been instrumental in defining the importance of this group:

Several studies have reported that mobile retirees generally fit the GRAMPIES profile. . . . These people are more active in lifestyle and consumption . . . are monied . . . are physically and psychologically in excellent shape.

1) More people are living longer.

2) More people are retiring earlier.

3) These people are more *active* in lifestyle and consumption.

4) These people are monied.

5) These people are physically and psychologically in excellent shape.

These retirees have an image of how they want to live in retirement and seek environments that facilitate that lifestyle. These sentiments are exemplified by the growing number of specialist retirement settlements, such as the Sun City and Leisure World communities, that have emerged in various parts of the country. These communities invariably emphasize in their promotion the array of opportunities they provide for engaging in recreation activities.

THE APPEAL OF RETIREES

In 1988, Alabama became the first state to organize a statewide program to attract retirees to relocate there. The initial program involved:

● placing advertisements in selected publications;

● compiling "how-to" handbooks on organizing local community retiree recruitment programs;

● initiating an 800 phone line and material to fulfill requests generated by it and the advertisements; and

● funding a cooperative brochure program.

Similar programs have since been launched by many other states, and there are now well over 100 local governments or chambers of commerce actively involved in attracting retirees (Longino 1995). One of these chambers of commerce with an active retirement marketing program reported receiving "250 to 500 requests a month for information about relocation here" (Smith 1994, B1).

The appeal of retirees to these government entities stems from their potential for stimulating local economies. If 100 retired households come to a community in a year, each with a retirement income of $40,000, their impact is similar to that of new business spending $4 million annually in the community.

Some communities are beginning to believe that retiree relocations may, in fact, be more desirable than business relocations. Social security and pension benefits of retirees are stable so their incomes are steady and not subject to the vicissitudes of economic business cycles. This income comes from outside the community, but retirees spend it locally so it stimulates the economy and generates jobs. Retirees not only increase the tax base, they tend to be positive taxpayers (Longino 1995); that is, they characteristically use fewer services than they pay for through taxes. For example, they pay taxes to school districts but do not send children there. Migrating retirees are not likely to strain social services, health care services, the local criminal justice system, or the natural environment.

There is a new, clean growth industry in America today—The industry is retirement migration.

Retirees transfer significant assets into local investment and banking institutions. For example, in Texas, the total annual net income (i.e., gains from in-migration assets minus losses from out-migration assets) from migrants age 60 and older between 1985 and 1990 averaged more than $150 million (Longino 1995). These assets expand the local deposit base that can be used for commercial and industrial financing. Retirees also provide the community with a pool of volunteers. They tend to be substantial contributors to and active in churches and local philanthropic and service organizations.

Older migrants are increasingly seen as economic saviors for some communities, especially in rural areas. This perception appears to be supported by empirical evidence. For example, Beale and Fuguitt (1990, 17) concluded that "retirement counties grew by 2 percent a year throughout the 1980s, twice the population growth rate of the total U.S. population." Similarly, Glasgow (1990) reported that retirement counties had the largest increases in personal income and employment among all nonmetropolitan counties.

Economic Research Services (1995, 18) have noted the potential costs associated with recruiting retirees:

> While generally viewed as a positive development for rural areas, the influx of retirees and other immigrants is not problem free. Increased demand for infrastructure (roads, water and sewer service, etc.) and social services, change in local cultural values, and escalation of property values and housing costs are among some of the factors associated with the trend that can be troublesome to long-term residents.

A particularly contentious issue is the belief that retirees vote against school funding. However, the research results on this question are ambiguous (Miller et al. 1994). Some studies support this belief (e.g., Voth and Danforth 1978; Button 1992), while other empirical investigations refute it (Button and Rosenbaum 1989).

Despite these caveats, it seems likely that Fox articulated the view that will gradually emerge in the coming years as conventional wisdom among those charged with the economic development of communities: "There is a new, clean growth industry in America today—The industry is retirement migration" (Foreword in Longino 1995, 7).

Capital improvements made as part of a retiree recruitment effort are likely to focus on such quality-of-life issues as recreational opportunities, beautification, ambience, or support services, which will also benefit existing residents.

From the perspective of economic development investments, targeting resources at recruiting retirees rather than exclusively at corporations has at least two major advantages. First, retirees do not require the economic incentive packages, comprised of such elements as tax abatements, low-interest loans, subsidized worker training programs, and infrastructure improvements, which are often standard prerequisites to a corporate relocation. Second, capital improvements made as part of a retiree recruitment effort are likely to focus on such quality-of-life issues as recreational opportunities, beautification, ambience, or support services, which will also benefit existing residents. Capital investments targeted at recruiting corporations involve large outlays for such things as developing industrial/business parks, access roads, and utilities. Local residents are likely to receive relatively little direct benefit from these facilities. Hence, the risk associated with recruiting corporations is higher because, if the corporate strategy fails, the community receives a much poorer return on its investment than if the strategy of attracting retirees fails.

THE ROLE OF RECREATION AMENITIES

The term "amenities" is an umbrella term that refers to those aspects of the environment in which retirees and others may find beauty, pleasure, and experiences that are unique to the locale (Siehl 1990). It is a popular belief that out-migration among retirees can be explained by the desire to move away from cold winters, but this is overly simplistic. The movement to the Sunbelt was noted earlier, but three of the major in-migration states, California, Florida, and Texas, were also among the top 10 states sending most out-migrants between 1985 and 1990.

Indeed, in terms of net gains and losses in the migration of the 60-and-older age cohort during that timeframe, California was a major net loser, with only New Jersey, Illinois, and New York having larger net out-migration in this age group among all 50 states. Clearly, more factors influence retiree movements than cold winters.

Extensive empirical evidence has been reported in the literature regarding the propensity of younger, affluent retirees to migrate to areas rich in amenities—particularly those with climate and recreational opportunities. The role of recreational opportunities is consistently reiterated. Carter (1988) noted a tendency among the younger elderly to move to areas that enabled them to enjoy their leisure pursuits with other elderly persons. Clifford et al. (1982) described an increase among the elderly making voluntary decisions to seek locations with more favorable climates and better recreational amenities. Fournier et al. (1988) referred to this segment of the elderly population as "footloose" amenity seekers, relatively unconstrained by economic forces. Fugitt and Tordella (1980) suggested that areas of rapid growth (in elderly population proportions) have been associated with recreational, physical, and geographic amenities. Heaton et al. (1980) commented on the leisure orientation of retired persons and their migration streams toward amenity-rich destinations. Kim and Hartswigen (1983) reported findings indicating that most moves among the elderly were related to the availability of amenities and their choice of lifestyle. The retiree sample used by Miller et al. (1994) was asked to review 14 features and indicate their importance in the decision to move. The first three in rank order were scenic beauty, recreational opportunities, and mild climate.

In her study of elderly movers, Biggar (1980) found that *local movers* usually selected "negatively," meaning they generally made involuntary moves within the same local areas because of a crisis (e.g., loss of spouse, declining income levels, or onset of health problems). Conversely, she reported that those who moved a greater distance characteristically cited "positive" attributes of the destination area as the reason for migrating. These migrants had higher socioeconomic levels. Thus, it was those with higher education and income levels who were "pulled" to areas they perceived to have greater opportunity (i.e., locations with more favorable climates, and better recreational, social, and health services).

In a subsequent paper, Biggar (1984) noted the expanding commercialization of recreation services and retirement communities, particularly in the Sunbelt, that offer a variety of different lifestyles from which to choose. She hailed elderly migrants as boons to the communities in which they relocate because they are consumers of housing and retail services, but do not place pressure on local job markets and social services.

Pampel et al. (1984) reported that climate, local living expenses, and travel time to relatives were the most significant factors in the relocation choices of their sample of aged persons.

They also noted, however, the rising importance of noneconomic amenities, such as climate, terrain, and recreational opportunities. Serow (1987) discovered a dichotomy of motives for residential relocation among older persons: (1) movement of younger, relatively affluent elderly persons to destinations based on climate and availability of amenities; and (2) movement of older elderly persons to destinations based on the availability of care and support.

Data . . . suggest that communities that fail to provide a high number of recreation opportunities for retirees are likely to have their tax base eroded by the loss of economic spending power from some of their more affluent retirees.

IMPLICATIONS

The literature reviewed in this chapter suggests that park and recreation amenities are a key ingredient in enticing relatively affluent retirees to migrate to a community. The converse of this is also likely to apply; that is, communities may lose their GRAMPIES if they fail to provide a comprehensive set of recreation opportunities comparable to those in other locations.

This finding was reported in a study of 270 individuals who had retired and migrated to permanently reside in the Texas Lower Rio Grande Valley area within the previous year (Haigood and Crompton 1998). These respondents were presented with 26 items known to potentially "push" people into migrating to another location from their resident community upon retirement. The two items on the list that referred to recreation were ranked second (desire to live in a more recreationally enjoyable area) and third (desire to live in a place where recreation opportunities are plentiful) in importance, behind desire to get away from cold weather. This suggests that wealthy retirees are likely to consider moving from communities that fail to provide a comprehensive set of recreation opportunities. Data from this study suggest that communities that fail to provide a high number of recreation opportunities for retirees are likely to have their tax base eroded by the loss of economic spending power from some of their more affluent retirees.

There is a strong social element in recreation. Indeed, a primary purpose of participating in recreation activities for many people is to facilitate socialization. Thus, encouraging retirees to stay in their home environment where there are extensive existing social networks should be easier for communities than recruiting to the area new retirees who face the formidable challenge of creating new social networks. If excellent recreation opportunities are available in the home environment, one of the primary reasons that retirees leave an area will disappear.

From an economic perspective, it is as important to retain existing retirees as to recruit new ones. If they fail to provide a comprehensive set of recreational opportunities comparable with those available in other locations, communities may lose their GRAMPIES. From this perspective, an agency can reposition its provision of services for retirees as being an investment in the community's economic health as well as in the personal well being of the beneficiaries of these services.

Afterword

The connection between parks and economic development was established early on in American urban park history, specifically by Olmsted's study of Central Park and its effect on surrounding property values, as John discusses in this report. It was, in fact, an argument used by park advocates in the late nineteenth and early twentieth centuries when many of this country's great urban parks were established.

It was a lesson seemingly forgotten during two world wars and the subsequent suburbanization of America. But recently, there has been a renewed interest in the impact of parks on real estate values and a community's overall economic development. The reason for this is twofold. First, it seems to be the impact that gets the attention of political and business leaders. It's much easier to sell a new or renovated park if you can show that it contributes financially to the community. Second, there is now a body of research and an emerging set of tools, such as John's excellent work here, to help park advocates prove that parks can positively affect economic development. This research support is crucial when vying for limited public and private investments.

There is a danger, though, in putting all our eggs into the economic benefits basket. During our first City Parks Forum (CPF) symposium in 1999, Mayor Tom Murphy of Pittsburgh, Pennsylvania, observed that "parks and many cultural events should not be forced into this kind of economic analysis mold but should have value for their own purpose. When we as mayors need to make decisions on the budget, if we're looking at cost-benefit like this, police, or fire, or other things are going to always win."

The mayor makes an excellent point. Parks will lose in many cost-benefit analyses. In Chapter 1, John identifies a number of the public benefits of parks and open space in addition to economic development. These benefits correlate to the issues identified by our participating mayors as some of the most pressing problems they face: crime and violence; education; public health; and infrastructure. One of the goals of CPF is to identify ways that parks and open space provide benefits related to those issues.

John also states the cardinal rule that park advocates should focus on only one or two benefits in aligning parks with community issues. Under that direction, it is imperative that the parks movement embrace research about as many park benefits as possible—not to use them all at once, but to maximize the flexibility of its advocacy. We must demonstrate that an investment in parks can provide not only economic development benefits, but social and environmental benefits as well (most of which ultimately have economic implications).

Unfortunately, there is little park-based empirical research on these subjects. The studies we do find usually come from other disciplines. For instance, a University of Illinois study showed that residents of housing projects landscaped with trees reported fewer incidents of domestic violence. A number of medical studies have shown the effects of viewing nature on human physiological responses, from reduced blood pressure and heart rates to pain control. A school principal in South Carolina reports that, following the installation of a "green" schoolyard, her students' test scores improved dramatically.

While these outcomes are significant and speak to how parks can potentially address urban problems, we need park-based research. Admittedly, this type of research presents several significant challenges. First, most park departments do not have the resources to conduct the necessary studies. Even if they did, many of these more "latent" benefits are not under the direct purview of the parks department. That is why it is critical for planners to play a role here, as they have the best opportunity to see the many interrelationships between parks and the quality of community life. Second, rigorous scientific research is challenged by the fact that parks exist in complex community settings, making it very difficult to isolate and control variables. And, finally, even the best research techniques and settings will have trouble overcoming the fact that many of the benefits of parks and open space are impossible to quantify.

How can we assign value to beauty, joy, or camaraderie? The answer is, we don't often try. Oddly, however, as John points out in this report, others (in particular, the nameless, faceless tourist "industry") have used images to create this relationship and reposition themselves. And others do this as well. Have you seen the credit card television commercials promoting their product as a way to capture the poignancy of human experience? The image on the television screen shows a dad and son at a baseball game while the voice-over states the cost of the ticket, the cost of the souvenir, and the cost of the hot dog. The voice goes on to state that the cost of the dad and son bonding experience is priceless. The concept of "priceless" is supposed to cause people to reach for a piece of plastic and spend money to make the experience possible. Of course, the ad is not really selling the experience (the baseball game could be a game other than a major league game, after all; no team is identified), it's selling the idea that you should use your credit card and run up a balance that causes you to pay the card company or the bank an interest charge, all in the name of the fact that some things are worth more than money. You better do those things now and not let money get in the way. Essentially, the card company or bank has repositioned itself from being a financial agency to being a facilitator of father/son bonding.

Ironically, the ad acknowledges that we all understand the "value" of the father/son experience and other experiences like it. We need to learn from that. Just because much of what we do is beyond any pricing scheme we can conceive, it doesn't mean that we give up entirely on determining the worth of the rest. It also doesn't mean that the appraisals that do allow us to put a dollar value on parks should alone drive our decisions; we should not become slaves to the bottom line. To do that would be to abandon our roots as a human service provider and sever us from the very reason that parks are public in the first place. No, we need to assign value to the benefits we can. And then we should just take credit for the rest. Like the tourism industry. Or better yet, a credit card marketing campaign.

Mary Eysenbach
Director, City Parks Forum

Appendix A. List of References

Allen, P. G., T. H. Stevens, and T. A. More. 1985. "Measuring the Economic Value of Urban Parks: A Caution." *Leisure Sciences* 7, no. 4: 467-77.

Beale, C., and G. Fuguitt. 1990. "Decade of Pessimistic Nonmetropolitan Population Trends Ends on Optimistic Note. *Rural Development Perspectives* 6:14-18.

Biggar, J. 1980. "Who Moved among the Elderly, 1965 to 1970." *Research on Aging* 2 (January): 73-91.

_____. 1984. "National Elderly Migration Patterns and Selectivity." *Research on Aging* 6 (February): 163-68.

Blair, J. P., and R. Premus. 1987. "Major Factors in Industrial Location: A Review." *Economic Development Quarterly* 1: 72-85.

Boyle, M. R. 1988. "Corporate Headquarters as Economic Development Targets." *Economic Development Review* 6: 50-56.

Bramlage, J. C. 1988. "All the Right Moves: A New Strategy for Successful Relocation." *Personnel* 65 (May): 40-43.

Brecher, Roth, and Edward Brecher. 1963. "Space for Everybody." *National Civic Review* October, 478-481, 488.

Bucknall, C. P. 1989. *The Real Cost of Development*. Poughkeepsie, N.Y.: Scenic Hudson Inc.

Button, J. W. 1992. "A Sign of Generational Conflict: The Impact of Florida's Aging Voters on Local School and Tax Referenda." *Social Science Quarterly* 73, no. 4: 786-97.

Button, J. W., and W. A. Rosenbaum. 1989. "Seeing Gray: School Bond Issues and The Aging in Florida." *Sage Publications* 11, no. 2: 158-73.

Carn, N. G., and J. Rabianski. 1991. "Selecting Industrial Locations, Sites." *National Real Estate Investor* 33, no. 24: 28-29.

Carter, J. 1988. "Elderly Local Migration." *Research on Aging* 10 (March): 99-119.

Clifford, W., T. Heaton, T., and G. Fugitt. 1982. "Residential Mobility and Living Arrangements Among The Elderly: Changing Patterns in Metropolitan and Nonmetropolitan Areas." *International Journal of Aging and Human Development* 14 (February): 139-56.

Conway, M. 1985. "The Megatech Industries: What Determines Their Location?" *Site Selection Handbook* 30: 626-35.

Cook, Ernest. 1994. "A Trust for Public Land Memorandum to Rand Wentworth, April 7." In Lerner, Steve, and William Poole. 1999. *The Economic Benefits of Parks and Open Spaces*. San Francisco: Trust for Public Land.

Crompton, J. L. 1999a. *Measuring The Economic Impact of Visitors to Sports Tournaments and Special Events*. Ashburn, Va.: National Recreation and Park Association.

_____. 1999b. *Strategic Options Available to the Trust For Public Land in Texas 2000-2004*. Austin, Tex.: Trust for Public Land.

_____. 2001a. "The Impact of Parks on Property Values: A Review of Empirical Evidence." *Journal of Leisure Research* 33, no. 1: 1-24.

_____. 2001b. "Perceptions of How the Presence of Greenway Trails Affects the Value of Proximate Properties." *Journal of Park and Recreation Administration* 19, no. 3: 33-51.

_____. 2001c. "Parks and Open Space: The Highest and Best Use of Land?" *Journal of Park and Recreation Administration* 19, no. 3: 133-154.

Crompton, J. L., L.L. Love, and T.A. More. 1997. "Characteristics of Companies that Considered Recreation/Parks/Open Space To Be Important in (Re)Location Decisions." *Journal of Park and Recreation Administration* 15, no. 1: 37-58.

Crossley, John C. 1986. *Public-commercial Cooperation in Parks and Recreation*. Columbus, Ohio: Publishing Horizons.

Decker, J. M., and J. L. Crompton. 1990. "Business Location Decisions: The Relative Importance of Quality of Life and Recreation, Park and Cultural Opportunities." *Journal of Park and Recreation Administration* 8, no. 2: 26-43.

_____. 1993. "Attracting Footloose Companies: An Investigation of the Business Location Process." *Journal of Professional Services Marketing* 9: 69-94.

Driver, B.L., and D.H. Bruns. 1999. "Concepts and Uses of the Benefits Approach to Leisure." In *Leisure Studies at the Millennium*, edited by T. Burton and E. Jackson. State College, Pa.: Venture Publishing.

Dugas, C. 1997. "Golf Drives Housing Trend." *USA Today*, 18 November, p. 1B.

Economic Research Service. 1995. *Understanding Rural America*. United States Department of Agriculture: Agricultural Information Bulletin, Number 710.

Epping, G. M. 1986. "Tradition in Transition: The Emergence of New Categories in Plant Location." *Arkansas Business and Economic Review* 19: 16-25.

Fagan, M., and C.F. Longino, Jr. 1993. "Migrating Retirees: A Source for Economic Development." *Economic Development Quarterly* 7: 98-106.

Festervand, T. A., J.R. Lumpkin, J. R., and D.S. Tosh. 1988. "Quality of Life in the Industrial Site Location Decision." *Journal of Real Estate Development* 4: 19-27.

Fournier, G., D. Rasmussen, D., and W. Serow. 1988. "Elderly Migration: For Sun and Money." *Population Research and Policy Review* 7: 189-99.

Fox, T. 1990. *Urban Open Space: An Investment that Pays*. New York: The Neighborhood Open Space Coalition.

Fugitt, G., and S. Tordella. 1980. "Elderly Net Migration." *Research on Aging* 2 (February): 191-204.

Galbraith, C., and A. F. DeNoble. 1988. "Location Decisions by High Technology Firms: A Comparison of Firm Size, Industry Type and Institutional Form." *Entrepreneurship: Theory and Practice* 13: 31-47.

Garvin, Alexander. 2000. *Parks, Recreation, and Open Space: A Twenty-First Century Agenda*. Planning Advisory Service Report No. 497/498. Chicago: APA.

Glaser, M., A., and J. W. Bardo. 1991. "The Impact of Quality of Life on Recruitment and Retention of Key Personnel." *American Review of Public Administration* 21: 57-72.

Glasgow, N. 1990. "Attracting Retirees as a Community Development Option." *Journal of the Community Development Society* 21: 102-14.

Godbey, G. 1993. "The Contribution of Recreation and Parks to Reducing Health Care Costs: From Theory to Practice." *Trends* 30, no. 4: 37-41.

Gunn, C. A. 1988. *Tourism Planning*. 2nd ed.. New York: Taylor and Francis.

Haigood, T. L., and J. L. Crompton. 1998. "The Role of Recreation Amenities in Retiree Relocation Decisions." *Journal of Park and Recreation Administration* 16, no. 1: 25-45.

Harding, C. F. 1989. "Location Choices for Research Labs: A Case Study Approach." *Economic Development Quarterly* 3: 223-34.

Harrison, B. 1994. "The Myth of Small Firs as the Predominant Job Generators." *Economic Development Quarterly* 8, no. 1: 3-18.

Haug, P., and P. Ness. 1993. "Industrial Location Decisions of Biotechnology Organizations." *Economic Development Quarterly* 7, no. 4: 390-420.

Heaton, T., W. Clifford, and G. Fugitt. 1980. "Changing Patterns of Retirement Migration." *Research on Aging* 2 (January): 93-104.

Howard, D. R., and J. L. Crompton. 1995. *Financing Sport*. Morgantown, W.V.: Fitness Information Technology.

Iso-Ahola, S. 1980. *The Social Psychology of Leisure and Recreation*. Dubuque, Iowa: Wm. C. Brown.

Kaplan, R., and S. Kaplan. 1990. *The Experience of Nature*. New York: Cambridge University Press.

Kim, J., and G. Hartswigsen. 1983. "The Current Population Shift among Elderly Migrants." *Research on Aging* 5 (February): 269-82.

Kotler, P., D. H. Haider, and I. Rein. 1993. *Marketing Places*. New York: The Free Press.

Lerner, Steve, and William Poole. 1999. *The Economic Benefits of Parks and Open Spaces.* San Francisco: Trust for Public Land.

Li, M. M., and H. J. Brown. 1980. "Micro-Neighborhood Externalities and Hedonic Housing Prices." *Land Economics* 56, no. 2: 125-41.

Little, C. E. 1990. *Greenways for America.* Baltimore, Md.: John Hopkins University Press.

Litwak, E., and C. Longino. 1987. "Migration Patterns among the Elderly: A Developmental Perspective." *The Gerontologist* 27 (March): 266-72.

Longino, C.F., Jr. 1995. *Retirement Migration in America.* Houston, Tex.: Vacation Publications.

Mahtesian, C. 1996. "Saving the States from Each Other." *Governing* (November): 15.

Marchant, Ward. 1995. "Open Range: Municipalities and Developers Coordinate Their Respective Interests to Fuel a Public Golf Boom in Colorado." *Golf Course Management* 63, no. 7: 41-42.

Martin, Douglas. 1994. "Trying New Ways to Save Decaying Parks." *New York Times,* November 15, A16.

McElyea, J. R., A.G. Anderson, and G.P. Krekorian. 1991. "Golf's Real Estate Value." *Urban Land* (February): 14-19.

Metropolitan Conference of City and State Park Authorities 1926. *Parks as Investments.* New York City. Cited in L.H.Weir. 1928. *Parks: A Manual of Municipal and County Parks.* New York: A.S. Barnes.

Miller, S. 1992. *The Economic Benefits of Open Space.* Islesboro, Me.: The Islesboro Islands Trust.

Miller, W., et al. 1994. *Retirement In-Migration Study.* Mississippi State, Miss.: Mississippi State University Southern Rural Development Center.

Murhead, D., and G. L. Rando. 1994. *Golf Course Development and Real Estate.* Washington D.C.: The Urban Land Institute.

Myers, D. 1987. "Internal Monitoring of Quality of Life for Economic Development." *Economic Development Quarterly* 1: 268-78.

Pampel, F., et al. 1984. "Retirement Migration Decision Making." *Research on Aging* 6 (February): 139-62.

Power, T. M. 1980. *The Economic Value of the Quality of Life.* Boulder, Colo.: Westview Press.

Rex, T. R. 1987. "Sixty Percent Might Leave Arizona; Quality of Life Key Factor." *Arizona Business* 34: 1-3.

Rogers, W. 1999. Introduction to *The Economic Benefits of Parks and Open Space* by Steve Lerner and William Poole. San Francisco: The Trust for Public Land.

Sarvis, M. J. 1989. "What to Look for in a New Office Facility." *Journal of Business Strategy* 10: 10-14.

Scanlon, J. R. 1984. "Site Selection and Design for the Growth Industries." *Industrial Development* 153: 26-29.

Selz, M. 1994. "More Businesses Set Up Shop in Western U.S." *Wall Street Journal,* 23 May, B1-B2.

Serow, W. 1987. "Why the Elderly Move." *Research on Aging* 9 (December): 582-97.

Siehl, G.H. 1990. *Amenity Resources and Rural Economic Growth: Report on a National Policy Symposium.* Washington D.C.: The Library of Congress, Congressional Research Service.

Simon, H. A. 1957. *Models of Man: Social And Rational: Mathematical Essays on Rational Human Behavior in a Social Setting.* New York: Wiley.

Smith, R.M. 1994. "Kerrville Ranks among Nation's Top 20 Retirement Locales." *Austin American Statesman,* 9 March, B1-B2.

Snepenger, D. J., J. D. Johnson, and R. Rasker. 1995. "Travel-Stimulated Entrepreneurial Migration." *Journal of Travel Research* 24, no. 1: 40-44.

Taylor, H. 1987. "Evaluating Our Quality of Life." *Industrial Development* (March/April): 1-4.

Tosh, D. S., T.A. Festervand, and J. R. Lumpkin. 1988. "Industrial Site Selection Criteria: Are Economic Developers, Manufacturers and Industrial Real Estate Brokers Operating on the Same Wave Length?" *Economic Development Review* 6: 62-67.

U.S. Bureau of the Census. 1989. "Population Profile of the U.S." *Current Population Reports, Special Studies, P23-159.* Washington, DC: U.S. Government Printing Office.

U.S. Bureau of the Census. 1992. "Sixty-five plus in America." *Current Population Reports, Special Studies, P23-178.* Washington, DC: U.S. Government Printing Office.

U.S. Department of Commerce. 1992. *Enterprise Statistics.* Table 3, Washington D.C.: U.S. Government Printing Office.

Van der Merwe, S. 1987. "GRAMPIES: A New Breed of Consumers Comes of Age." *Business Horizons* (November-December): 14-19.

Voth, D.E, and D.M. Danforth. 1978. *Consequences of Migration into Arkansas for Population Change.* Fayetteville, Ark: Agricultural Experiment Station, Bulletin 855.

Warnes, A. 1982. *Geographical Perspectives on the Elderly.* New York: John Wiley and Sons, Inc.

Wiatrowski, W. J. 2001. "Changing Retirement Age: Ups and Downs." *Monthly Labor Review* (April): 3-12.

Winton, Pete. 1994. "Developers Scramble for Shot at Public Golf Course." *Fort Myers News-Press*, August 3, 1, 16.

Wiseman, R. 1980. "Why Older People Move." *Research on Aging* 2 (February): 141-54.

Wiseman, R., and C. Roseman. 1979. "A Typology of Elderly Migration Based on the Decision-Making Process." *Economic Geography* 55 (April): 324-37.

MAKING GREAT COMMUNITIES HAPPEN

The American Planning Association provides leadership in the development of vital communities by advocating excellence in community planning, promoting education and citizen empowerment, and providing the tools and support necessary to effect positive change.

452. Saving Face: How Corporate Franchise Design Can Respect Community Identity. Ronald Lee Fleming. June 1994. 72pp. $30; PAS subscribers $15.

454. Design Review. Mark L. Hinshaw. February 1995. 34pp. $28; PAS subscribers $14.

455. Neighborhood-Based Planning: Five Case Studies. Wendelyn A. Martz. March 1995. 34pp. $28; PAS subscribers $14.

456. Traffic Calming. Cynthia L. Hoyle. July 1995. 28pp. $28; PAS subscribers $14.

457/458. A Guide to Wellhead Protection. Jon Witten and Scott Horsley with Sanjay Jeer and Erin K. Flanagan. August 1995. 104pp. $34; PAS subscribers $17.

459. Bicycle Facility Planning. Suzan Anderson Pinsof and Terri Musser. October 1995. 44pp. $32; PAS subscribers $16.

460. Preparing a Conventional Zoning Ordinance. Charles A. Lerable. December 1995. 61pp. $34; PAS subscribers $17.

461. Performance Standards in Growth Management. Douglas Porter, ed. January 1996. 44pp. $32; PAS subscribers $16.

462/463. Modernizing State Planning Statutes: The Growing Smart℠ Working Papers. Volume 1. March 1996. 190pp. $24; PAS subscribers $12.

464. Planners' Salaries and Employment Trends. Marya Morris. July 1996. 25pp. $28; PAS subscribers $14.

465. Adequate Public Facilities Ordinances and Transportation Management. S. Mark White. August 1996. 80pp. $34; PAS subscribers $17.

466. Planning for Hillside Development. Robert B. Olshansky. November 1996. 50pp. $32; PAS subscribers $16.

467. A Planners Guide to Sustainable Development. Kevin J. Krizek and Joe Power. December 1996. 66pp. $32; PAS subscribers $16.

468. Creating Transit-Supportive Land-Use Regulations. Marya Morris, ed. December 1996. 76pp. $34; PAS subscribers $17.

469. Gambling, Economic Development, and Historic Preservation. Christopher Chadbourne, Philip Walker, and Mark Wolfe. March 1997. 56pp. $32; PAS subscribers $16.

470/471. Habitat Protection Planning: Where the Wild Things Are. Christopher J. Duerksen, Donald L. Elliott, N. Thompson Hobbs, Erin Johnson, and James R. Miller. May 1997. 82pp. $34; PAS subscribers $17.

472. Converting Storefronts to Housing: An Illustrated Guide. July 1997. 88pp. $34; PAS subscribers $17.

473. Subdivision Design in Flood Hazard Areas. Marya Morris. September 1997. 62pp. $32; PAS subscribers $16.

474/475. Online Resources for Planners. Sanjay Jeer. November 1997. 126pp. $34; PAS subscribers $17.

476. Nonpoint Source Pollution: A Handbook for Local Governments. Sanjay Jeer, Megan Lewis, Stuart Meck, Jon Witten, and Michelle Zimet. December 1997. 127pp. $32; PAS subscribers $16.

477. Transportation Demand Management. Erik Ferguson. March 1998. 68pp. $32; PAS subscribers $16.

478. Manufactured Housing: Regulation, Design Innovations, and Development Options. Welford Sanders. July 1998. 120pp. $32; PAS subscribers $16.

479. The Principles of Smart Development. September 1998. 113pp. $32; PAS subscribers $16.

480/481. Modernizing State Planning Statutes: The Growing Smart℠ Working Papers. Volume 2. September 1998. 269pp. $28; PAS subscribers $14.

482. Planning and Zoning for Concentrated Animal Feeding Operations. Jim Schwab. December 1998. 44pp. $32; PAS subscribers $16.

483/484. Planning for Post-Disaster Recovery and Reconstruction. Jim Schwab, et al. December 1998. 346pp. $34; PAS subscribers $17.

485. Traffic Sheds, Rural Highway Capacity, and Growth Management. Lane Kendig with Stephen Tocknell. March 1999. 24pp. $26; PAS subscribers $13.

486. Youth Participation in Community Planning. Ramona Mullahey, Yve Susskind, and Barry Checkoway. June 1999. 70pp. $32. PAS subscribers $16.

487/488. Crossroads, Hamlet, Village, Town: Design Characteristics of Traditional Neighborhoods, Old and New. Randall Arendt. September 1999. 144pp. $34; PAS subscribers $17.

489/490. Aesthetics, Community Character, and the Law. Christopher J. Duerksen and R. Matthew Goebel. December 1999. 154pp. $34; PAS subscribers $17.

491/492. A Glossary of Zoning, Development, and Planning Terms. Edited by Michael Davidson and Fay Dolnick. December 1999. 261pp. $34; PAS subscribers $17.

493. Transportation Impact Fees and Excise Taxes: A Survey of 16 Jurisdictions. Connie B. Cooper. July 2000. 62pp. $32; PAS subscribers $16.

494. Incentive Zoning: Meeting Urban Design and Affordable Housing Objectives. Marya Morris. September 2000. 64pp. $32; PAS subscribers $16.

495/496. Everything You Always Wanted To Know About Regulating Sex Businesses. Eric Damian Kelly and Connie Cooper. December 2000. 168pp. $34; PAS subscribers $17.

497/498. Parks, Recreation, and Open Spaces: An Agenda for the 21st Century. Alexander Garvin. December 2000. 72pp. $34; PAS subscribers $17.

499. Regulating Home-Based Businesses in the Twenty-First Century. Charles Wunder. December 2000. 37pp. $32; PAS subscribers $16.

500/501. Lights, Camera, Community Video. Cabot Orton, Keith Spiegel, and Eddie Gale. April 2001. 76pp. $34; PAS subscribers $17.

502. Parks and Economic Development. John L. Crompton. November 2001. 74pp. $34; PAS subscribers $17.

CPSIA information can be obtained at www.ICGtesting.com
Printed in the USA
LVOW032340180112

264340LV00002B/3/P